What They *Really* Said series
*Edited by* A. N. GILKES

WHAT SHAW *REALLY* SAID

RUTH ADAM

# WHAT
# SHAW
# *REALLY*
# SAID

Schocken Books · New York

Published in the United States of America in 1966
by Schocken Books Inc., 67 Park Avenue, New York, N.Y. 10016

Library of Congress Catalog Card No. 66-24901
Manufactured in the United States of America

This book is dedicated to my brother, R. Wearing King, with my sincere gratitude for his expert and most valuable advice on many points in connection with it.

# Contents

# Contents

# Acknowledgments

The author and the publishers wish to express their thanks to the Public Trustee and the Society of Authors for permission to quote from the works of Bernard Shaw.

# I  Shaw's Life-Story

When George Bernard Shaw died, his housekeeper went out to tell the waiting reporters at the garden gate; the cars and motor-cycles started up and rushed off and within minutes the announcement was flashing round the globe. It arrested the whole civilized world. In New York, the lights of Broadway were darkened as a sign of mourning. In Australia, theatre audiences stood for two minutes' silence. In India, the cabinet adjourned. The Swedes delivered a formal note of condolence to the British ambassador. Presidents, prime ministers and outstanding men of letters laid everything else aside in order to try to condense what he had meant, as social revolutionary and author, into a few quotable sentences. Perhaps Nehru of India most nearly succeeded when he said, "Shaw was not only one of the greatest figures of the age but one who influenced the thoughts of vast numbers of human beings during two generations."

Next morning the papers gave the news of his death the place of honour and printed the obituaries which had been waiting for half a century in their files. He had written political pamphlets, criticism, novels and sixty plays. He left one of the largest fortunes ever earned by a writer. He had been offered the Nobel prize, refused the Order of Merit and a peerage, had a dramatic festival established for his works, helped to create the British Labour Party and become a legend during his own lifetime. He had lived through three major wars and six reigns and was personally responsible for much of the difference between nineteenth-century thinking and that of the twentieth.

Like Shakespeare, his name was adapted to add a new adjective to the English language. "Shavian" is defined by the Oxford dictionary as "Characteristic of Bernard Shaw". It is a unique way of looking at life and the universe, a way conceived in the mind of an obscure Irish boy, born in the middle of the nineteenth century and so influencing the twentieth that for fifty years before his death and for generations after it ordinary people would ask each other, when faced with a problem, "Didn't Bernard Shaw once say . . .?" Did he say that all great truths begin as blasphemies? That virtue is only the trades-unionism of the married? That the worst of crimes is poverty? That all professions are conspiracies against the laity? That if you strike a child you should strike it in anger? That all progress depends on the unreasonable man?

### Childhood

Shaw was born in 1856, in Dublin, into what he called the Downstart class—a family going down in the world but clinging desperately to its social position. The Shaws came from the lower reaches of the Protestant hierarchy which ran Ireland and looked down on the Roman Catholic majority as politically and socially inferior and as Papists destined to damnation in any case. His father was a minor civil servant, later an unsuccessful corn merchant. His mother was the daughter of a country gentleman. She married beneath her quite deliberately as the only way of getting away from home and found out, on her honeymoon, that her husband was a confirmed drunkard. Bernard Shaw and his two elder sisters were left to servants (at £8 a year) in childhood and to guide themselves as best they could in adolescence. When he was sixteen, his mother broke up her home and went to live in London.

But in this unpromising background the amiable virtues which distinguished Shaw all his life grew and flourished like weeds. He had no chip on his shoulder. He was generous-hearted and unjudging, so that petty spite and malice were incomprehensible to him. He never could believe that the people with whom he quarrelled actually went on nursing their resentment for years afterwards. His most remembered play-characters—such as Caesar and Joan of Arc—have a large nobility of spirit which only a completely tolerant writer could invent. Only one character, out of all his plays, is wholly hateful, and that is a woman who broke the spirit of her children by "godly tyranny".

Shaw's own mother, whom he described as "a Bohemian anarchist with ladylike habits", neglected her children, partly through inefficiency but also because she was determined they should not be nagged and bullied as she

had been as a child. She gave him a love for and understanding of music which lasted all his life. Her household
was chiefly remarkable for fecklessness, self-indulgence
and petty snobbery. But it had a natural kindliness and
gentleness, a careless good-nature which is perhaps only
possible in an Irish home. She was not in the least bitter
about her husband. "She took him as he was, in kindly
Irish fashion, without trumping up a moral case against
him. We were all like that, more or less." She and her
children left him in the end, without recriminations, but
simply because he was no kind of a support to them. "In
doing so, we took off his shoulders a burden he was unable
to bear and glad to discard." But all the same he sent them
a pound a week which he could ill afford until he died.

Shaw discovered that his father was a drunkard when
"I was about as tall as his boots. The wrench from my
childish faith in my father, as perfect and omniscient, to
the discovery that he was a hypocrite and a dipsomaniac
was so sudden and violent that it must have left its mark
on me." All the same he was a kindly and likeable man.
He had a passion for comic anti-climax which his son
inherited and loved to include in the plays. When the boy
Bernard Shaw scoffed at the Bible his father gave him a
long lecture on ignorance and irreverence, told him that
the Bible was a literary and historical masterpiece and
ended by adding, with an air of perfect fairness, that the
worst enemy of religion could say no worse of the Bible
than that it was the damndest parcel of lies ever written.

Shaw went to a succession of cheap schools and left at
fifteen. There was no hope of his family being able to
afford to send him to the university. He got a job in a
land-agent's office at £18 a year. At twenty he decided to

leave Ireland and join his mother in London, because "I am not enamoured of failure, of poverty and obscurity and of the ostracism and contempt which these imply; and these were all that Dublin offered to the enormity of my conscious ambition."

## In the Wilderness

In London he lived with his mother and surviving sister in a semi-detached house off the Brompton Road. His mother earned some money by teaching music, his sister by singing and they had a small inheritance on which they could draw. Shaw did odd jobs but spent his energy on learning to be a writer. He wrote five novels and got sixty publishers' refusals for them. Every day he filled five pages of quarto and if the fifth page ended in the middle of a sentence he left it there until next day. He was poor and shabby and agonizingly shy. Before he could bring himself to go out anywhere he went to the British Museum and studied a book of etiquette, *The Manners and Tone of Good Society*. He joined a debating club and made up his mind to learn public speaking, forcing himself to take every opportunity to make a speech "like an officer afflicted with cowardice who takes every opportunity of going under fire to get over it and learn his business".

He went to hear Henry George speak on Land Nationalization and from there to the Museum to study Karl Marx's *Das Kapital*. This was a turning-point in his life. It converted him to Socialism, provided him with a mission and made him a revolutionary writer. For twelve years he spoke three times a week for the Cause, at street-corners and in halls, at the dock gates and at the British Association. He became known as an orator. He joined the newly-formed Fabian Society and persuaded his friend Sidney Webb to join. "He was extraordinarily able and quite respectable. I was a futile Bohemian. He was an indefatigable investigator. I was an intuitive guesser." Together they remodelled the society which eventually became the cradle of the Labour Party.

In 1885, when Shaw was twenty-nine, William Archer, the dramatic critic, noticed him in the British Museum, absorbed in a French translation of Karl Marx, with the score of Wagner's *Tristan and Isolde* open beside it. They became friends, and Archer arranged for Shaw to work as a critic. After nine years' penury he found himself with an income of £117 a year. Archer introduced him to the works of Henrik Ibsen, the revolutionary Norwegian dramatist. This was the second turning-point in Shaw's life.

He developed a passion for "Ibsenism" and took to attacking Shakespeare—or rather the Shakespeare cult —"Bardolatry" as he called it. He became established as a controversial critic of music, art and the theatre. "My fame at once increased with a rush; and thenceforth for many years my name seldom appeared in print without the adjective brilliant, which I disliked, as it suggested a glittering superficiality."

He experimented with play-writing in the Ibsen manner himself. In 1892 his first play *Widowers' Houses*—about slum-landlordism—was produced. His second play was turned down by all London managers and his third, *Mrs Warren's Profession*, an exposure of prostitution, was turned down by the censor. Before the end of the century he was critic, playwright, Fabian and a borough councillor for St. Pancras all at once. Through the Webbs he met an Irish Fabian, Charlotte Payne-Townshend, with "light green eyes and a million of money". She acted as his secretary. While she was abroad, he fell ill. She came home to look after him and stayed to marry him.

## Success

Shaw's years in the wilderness ended with the century. He had begun to write comedies, "pleasant plays", and to listen to the actor-managers who dominated the theatre and knew exactly what they wanted in the way of a piece which would be a commercial success and provide them with a good part. Shaw gave them what they asked, but in his own way—using Ibsen's realism about social problems but doing it with laughter instead of Scandinavian gloom. He introduced intellectual debate into his stories. Audiences listened, just as a man in a railway-carriage will put down the most exciting novel in order to listen to an argument which has broken out. Shaw also revived the idea of including a long preface, explaining what the play was about, in the published version.

It was the Royal Court Theatre which established him as a dramatist. Between 1904 and 1907 it had an experimental management, which put on new plays as fast as he could write them. They made the same kind of impact as the "kitchen-sink" school was to have there half a century later, but more important because in the early nineteen-hundreds the legitimate stage had the field to itself, without the rivalry of films, radio and television. Audiences and critics were by turns shocked, delighted, furious and amused. The king came to *Arms and the Man* and frowned, to *John Bull's Other Island* and laughed so much that he broke his chair.

When Shaw wrote *Man and Superman* about his own idea of creative evolution he became the idol of young English intellectuals, though he made more money out of it in America than in Britain. In the last few years before the 1914 war his plays graduated from the Court and repertory productions to the West End proper. *Pygmalion* finally established him as the most popular playwright in the country.

When war broke out he fell from the height of his popularity to the most unpopular period of his whole life. He had helped the Webbs to found the *New Statesman*. In 1914 he wrote a manifesto for it, "Common-Sense About the War," examining Britain's case dispassionately and pointing out that there were as many hypocrites and militarists in England as in Germany and remarking that one way of arresting the universal madness would be for the soldiers of every army to shoot their officers and go home. It was the time of the 1914 "war fever", which was worse than any hysteria of the 1939 war. Shaw's old friends steered clear of him and acquaintances cut him dead in public. The press suggested that his plays should be boycotted and Herbert Asquith said that he ought to be shot. His letter-box was crammed with abuse by every post. "As I employ a lady-secretary, I published a request that my correspondents should write the word 'Obscene' on the top left-hand corner of their envelopes." He finished *Heartbreak House*—a picture of contemporary England—and began *Back to Methuselah*, a play-cycle about the future of the human race. Both were produced in the early twenties, by which time the British had become disillusioned about the glory of war and were prepared to admire him again.

## The Summit

Then came his masterpiece, *Saint Joan*. It was first produced in New York in 1923, then in London in 1924, with Sybil Thorndike as the Maid. It ran for 244 performances, has been regularly revived since, admired by Catholics, Protestants and atheists alike, made (inadequately) into a film and—contrary to Shaw's passionate plea that his works should not be made instruments of torture so that he would be hated as Shakespeare is hated by children—used as a school textbook.

## The Sage

During his last quarter-century he was regarded as the sage of the western world. Playgoers made pilgrimages to the Malvern Festival, where his new plays could be seen. Tourists haunted Ayot St. Lawrence, the village in which he lived, hoping to get a glimpse of the great man. Everything he said, during these years, was news, and a comment from him about any important event was always looked for first. He had a set of printed postcards to use as replies to correspondents and a special one for editors. ("Mr. Bernard Shaw is willing, when time permits, to answer written questions when they happen to be interesting as current news and can be answered in twenty words or less. Questions that require answers at greater length should be accompanied by an offer of a fee of not less than three figures.") Postcards on which he had scrawled a postscript himself became collectors' pieces.

He wrote one study of Socialism, one of established religions and half a dozen socio-political plays. He had begun to concentrate on discussion rather than drama, and only one of these later plays has lived on after the current topics they dealt with have been forgotten.

During the 1939–45 war he occasionally broke into the news again, saying that Britain had only herself to thank for the rise of Hitler and that the future lay with Stalin, but the public by now cherished his perversity and was amused and satisfied that he was still in his old form, rather than indignant. His wife died. The war ended. He wrote some biographical sketches about himself, scolded and corrected his many biographers for their inaccuracies, sometimes threatened to have visitors thrown out or received them with benevolent courtesy, unpredictably, made a will leaving money and detailed directions for the foundation of a new English alphabet and died, as a result of a fall in his garden, on All Souls' Day in November, 1950. He was ninety-four.

William Temple once asked his father why philosophers did not rule the world. The Archbishop replied, "They do rule it years after they are dead." But—particularly during the first decades after their death—they are often misquoted, misrepresented and misinterpreted. Shaw said that he was a hopeless subject for a biographer because there was nothing interesting to be said about him that he had not already said about himself and that what he had to say was more interesting than his personal adventures. "Things have not happened to me; on the contrary it is I who have happened to them: and all my happenings have taken the form of books and plays. Read them or spectate them and you have my whole story." It is what Shaw really said that matters, not what he did or what he is supposed to have meant.

What did Shaw really say?

# 2   About God

Shaw said, "I am religious enough to have spent a great part of my life trying to clean up the heavily barnacled creeds and make them credible."

*Making of an Agnostic*
Shaw's religious training supplied all the ingredients most likely to produce a fully-fledged atheist. His parents supported their church entirely for the sake of social status. His religious instruction consisted of learning texts by heart and being forced to sit through a long dull service without ever feeling personally involved. He spent the time wishing they would sing something out of an opera instead of hymns. His nursemaid told him to say "cold" prayers (beside the bed, not in it) otherwise God would not hear. His uncle told him that the raising of Lazarus was a ruse, arranged beforehand by Lazarus and

Jesus. At twelve years old Shaw became an atheist. He experienced the sense of relief common to all who liberate themselves from a set of forced and unreal beliefs. But one question-mark remained. In the same moment that he denied the existence of God he became conscious of what he called "moral passion" in himself. The Quakers call it the "inner light". Shaw said, "My soul was born of that passion." It would not fit into atheism.

In after life he looked back and decided that it was lucky for him that he had been made to realize the absurdities of established religion so early because it had driven him to search for a real religion. The search was not finished when he died.

He began by attacking the God of Victorian convention —"that old tribal idol called Jehovah"—who, he said, demanded blood-sacrifices, watched out for chances of petty revenge and arranged for his son to be horribly executed in order to make up for his father's misdeed in not creating a more successful human race. Once, at a Kensington party, Shaw publicly challenged Jehovah to strike him dead within five minutes if he really existed and disapproved of atheism. The challenge created equal nervousness among the sceptics present and the faithful. At his host's request he withdrew it before the five minutes were up.

At that time atheism was the fashionable creed among intellectual rebels. It had started with Darwin's *Origin of Species*, which proved that all species had evolved, not been created in the literal fashion of the Bible story. But Shaw soon became impatient with the earnest atheists. He said that what sensible people want to know is what you believe, not what you do not believe. He told the National Secular Society that any clever Jesuit could out-argue them. Rationalism, he decided, stopped short of the most important question. "Reason can discover the best way—bus or underground or taxi—to get from Piccadilly Circus to Putney, but it cannot explain why you should want to go to Putney instead of staying in Piccadilly." A child's first questions, he said, are "What? Where? When? How? Why?" Secular science can answer the first three and partly answer the fourth. "But the fifth—'Why?'—is absolute checkmate to the scientist." Darwin had explained how man had evolved from the monkey; but not why he should have done so.

Shaw put the question into dramatic form. He wrote *The Devil's Disciple*. This was a melodrama, based on a set of traditional stage situations which playgoers expected and liked; a dead man's will; an oppressed orphan who finds a protector; a hero who makes a heroic sacrifice and is court-martialled but reprieved at the last moment. But he used the old formula to carry a new idea. The Devil's Disciple is a man who has turned his back on God because he was brought up under the tyranny of the old tribal idol Jehovah. (In this play the hero's mother is the only entirely unsympathetic character of Shaw's works.) But the hero is trapped, in spite of himself, by his own soul, or inner light, or "moral passion". Unaccountably he finds himself offering his life for a stranger.

RICHARD. I had no motive and no interest; all I can tell you is that when it came to the point whether I would take my neck out of the noose and put another man's into it, I could not do it. I don't know why not: I see myself as a fool for my pains: but I could not and I cannot. I have been brought up standing by the law of my own nature: and I may not go against it, gallows or no gallows.

Thirteen years later Shaw used the same formula to illustrate the same idea in *The Shewing-Up of Blanco Posnet*. But by then he was beginning to find his own answer to his own question. The horse-thief, Blanco, who stayed to save a child's life when he could have got away, knows that he has been driven to it by God, but not, he persists, by the kind of God he was taught about in Sunday-school.

Shaw himself described this play as a religious tract in dramatic form. The censor described it as blasphemous and banned it. The point of controversy was Blanco's description of the Almighty who has inspired him to be better than he wanted to be.

BLANCO. He's a sly one. He's a mean one. He lies low for you. He plays cat and mouse with you. He lets you run loose until you think youre shut of Him and then when you least expect it, He's got you.

## The Life Force

In the course of seventy-four writing years, Shaw said so much on the subject of religion that his biographers come to different conclusions about what he really believed. They find apparent contradictions—for instance in the worn Bible, marked "My travelling Bible", in his study and his will which forbade that there should be any religious service for him after his death. The reason for the paradoxes in his writing is that he never reached a cut-and-dried formula which fitted any of the established religions, but went on trying to work out a faith which would stand up to the test of freethinking, and which he could accept intellectually and philosophically. Two distinct lines of thought are the most important. One is about God the creator, the Mind behind evolution. The other is about Christianity as a way of life.

He found a name for the Mind, the Life Force, and built a play around the idea—*Man and Superman.* It tries to answer the question which Darwin had left unanswered—*why* should the species evolve? Why should the monkey not be content to remain a monkey, but struggle up into a higher form of life which was Man? And was Man also struggling upward? Shaw thought so. The hero of *Man and Superman* is a brilliant, original, intellectual and revolutionary, determined not to be trapped into marriage but to keep his freedom. In a dream he becomes Don Juan, the legendary seducer of women. Don Juan has died and gone to hell, which turns out to be not a place of torture but of intolerable emptiness and boredom, because it is full of shallow and lazy people who will not use their abilities as the Life Force intended them to. Don Juan realizes that his chief talents—his intellect and virility and sexual prowess—were meant to be used to further Evolution, to help the Superman, who will be the next stage of man, to evolve. When the hero wakes and returns to the real world, he understands that what he has to do is to submit to marriage even though it means giving up his freedom. "This is the true joy in life, the being used for a purpose recognized by yourself as a mighty one; the being thoroughly worn out before you are thrown on the scrap heap; the being a force of Nature instead of a feverish selfish little clod of ailments and grievances, complaining that the world will not devote itself to making you happy." But the Life Force makes itself felt in other directions besides sex and the further-ance of its plans for evolution. The philosopher who is able to understand its purposes and explain them is also obeying it. As Don Juan explains to the irritated Devil:

DON JUAN. The philosopher is in the grip of the Life Force. This Life Force says to him "I have done a thousand wonderful things unconsciously by merely willing to live and following the line of least resistance; now I want to know myself and my destination and choose my path; so I have made a special brain—a philosopher's brain—to grasp this knowledge for me as the husbandman's hand grasps the plough for me."

Shaw believed that the artist who uses his talent, the explorer who uses his, and the reformer are all fulfilling the purpose for which the Life Force created them. So is the hero, who offers his life in obedience to "an urge to self-sacrifice against all the dictates of common-sense". The action of one who gives his life for a stranger or an ideal can only be explained by the existence of some power outside and above human beings. Such actions are not inspired by ordinary human love. If you want to find out about the deeds done for love, you do not look at the stories of heroes who won medals for heroism, but in the police-court news of assault and murder.

## Christianity
One of Shaw's gibes at those who attacked his religious theories was that they had not really studied the Bible as he had, but were relying on second-hand information and

the superstitions of conventional religion. In *Androcles and the Lion* he took the conventional Christian-martyr play—of the *Quo Vadis* type—and used it to illustrate the idea that the early Christians were persecuted because they were so unconventional and would not subscribe to the established traditional religion of their time. A Roman officer gives them a last chance to conform.

THE CAPTAIN. All that is necessary is to sacrifice to the gods: a simple and convenient ceremony effected by dropping a pinch of incense on the altar, after which the prisoner is at once set free. Under such circumstances you have only your own perverse folly to blame if you suffer. I suggest to you that if you cannot burn a morsel of incense as a matter of conviction, you might at least do so as a matter of good taste, to avoid shocking the religious convictions of your fellow citizens. I am aware that these considerations do not weigh with Christians; but it is my duty to call your attention to them.

He tries to persuade one of the Christian prisoners, with whom he is beginning to fall in love, that she will be making a useless sacrifice.

THE CAPTAIN (*rather troubled, addressing her personally and gravely*). A martyr, Lavinia, is a fool. Your death will prove nothing.
LAVINIA. Then why kill me?
THE CAPTAIN. I mean that truth, if there be any truth, needs no martyrs.
LAVINIA. No; but my faith, like your sword, needs testing. Can you test your sword except by staking your life on it?
THE CAPTAIN (*suddenly resuming his official tone*). I call the attention of the female prisoner to the fact that

Christians are not allowed to draw the Emperor's officers into arguments and put questions to them for which the military regulations provide no answer.

In this play Shaw achieves what most fiction-writers find impossibly difficult, that is to make goodness attractive. Androcles—the slave who is thrown to the lions, but saved by meeting the one which he had once succoured by taking a thorn out of its paw—is a far more engaging character than any portrayal of that other Christian animal-lover, St. Francis of Assisi. As he waits to die, he is told sadistically that the lion has been starved to make it more savage.

ANDROCLES. I'm glad he's hungry. Not that I want him to suffer, poor chap! but then he'll enjoy eating me so much more. Theres a cheerful side to everything.

All the other characters find it impossible not to love Androcles. Even the hardened Coliseum official, the Editor, whose job it is to put the circus on, tries to save him from martyrdom.

THE EDITOR (*rising and striding over to Androcles*). Here; dont you be obstinate. Come with me and drop the pinch of incense on the altar. Thats all you need do to be let off.

ANDROCLES. No: thank you very much indeed; but I really mustnt.

THE EDITOR. What! Not to save your life?

ANDROCLES. I'd rather not. I couldnt sacrifice to Diana; she's a huntress, you know, and kills things.

THE EDITOR. That dont matter. You can choose your own altar. Sacrifice to Jupiter: he likes animals; he turns himself into an animal when he goes off duty.

ANDROCLES. No: it's very kind of you; but I feel I cant save myself that way.

Androcles is only roused to anger when a slave is sent to lash one of the Christians into fighting, that is, to torture him into breaking his vow of non-resistance.

*The Call Boy returns with a man in a hideous Etruscan mask, carrying a whip. They both rush down the passage into the arena.*

ANDROCLES (*scrambling to his feet and running into the middle of the space between the staircases*). It's dreadful. Now *I* want to fight. I cant bear the sight of a whip. The only time I ever hit a man was when he lashed an old horse with a whip. It was terrible. I danced on his face when he was on the ground. He mustnt strike Ferrovius. I'll go into the arena and kill him first. (*He makes a wild dash into the passage.*)

Ferrovius (who has in fact killed all six gladiators single-handed, before Androcles gets there) is the type of Christian whom Shaw disliked, a conscience-ridden "Pauline Christian", who believes in sudden conversions and achieves them by strong-arm methods. He is a man of immense physical strength, a born fighter, who finds non-violence difficult. Before he was sent into the arena, he had an angry dispute with the Editor.

FERROVIUS (*curbing himself by a mighty effort*). Oh, my temper, my wicked temper! (*To the Editor*) Forgive me, brother. My heart was full of wrath: I should have been thinking of your dear precious soul.
THE EDITOR. Yah! (*He turns his back on Ferrovius contemptuously, and goes back to his seat*).

FERROVIUS (*continuing*). And I forgot it all: I thought of nothing but offering to fight you with one hand tied behind me.

THE EDITOR (*turning pugnaciously*). What!

FERROVIUS (*on the border line between zeal and ferocity*). Oh, dont give way to pride and wrath, brother. I could do it so easily.

Shaw's martyrs, he says, are the martyrs of all time, "people who are shown by their inner light the possibility of a better world based on the demand of the spirit for a nobler and more abundant life, not for themselves at the expense of others, but for everybody." They may have different enthusiasms—different ways of holding their religion—but they will always be opposed by the official one.

The martyr in the play who most nearly represents Shaw's own religious sense is Lavinia, who is a young patrician woman, a fearless freethinker. The Roman captain argues with her that the exact name of the true God does not matter and that she can drop her incense saying to herself that she is doing it for her own God.

THE CAPTAIN. Call him what you will as you drop the incense on the altar flame; He will understand.

LAVINIA. No. I couldnt. That is the strange thing, Captain, that a little pinch of incense should make all that difference. Religion is such a great thing that when I meet really religious people, we are friends at once, no matter what name we give to the divine will that made us and moves us. Oh, do you think that I, a woman, would quarrel with you for sacrificing to a woman god like Diana, if Diana meant to you what Christ means to me? No: we should kneel side by side before her altar like two children. But when men who believe neither in my god nor in their own—men who do not know the meaning of the word religion—when these men drag me to the foot of an iron statue that has become the symbol of the terror and darkness through which they walk, of their cruelty and greed, of their hatred of God and their oppression of man—when they ask me to pledge my soul before the people that this hideous idol is God, and that all this wickedness and falsehood is divine truth, I cannot do it, not if they could put a thousand cruel deaths on me.

The other articulate martyr is Spintho, a neurotic debauchee. Shaw points out that all revolutionary movements attract some of those who are not good enough for established organizations, as well as those who are too good for them; and Spintho is the illustration. He has joined because he is afraid of death, and believes that martyrs are certain of eternal life. He is the Christian whose faith depends on the stories and dreams, the comforts of Christianity, but when it comes to the real test, the stories and dreams melt away and he recants.

In the preface to *Androcles*, Shaw examines the faith of his martyrs. He argues that what is generally accepted as Christianity is something quite apart from the specific doctrine of Christ. It is built up out of the common rituals of primitive religions. The god, or Corn King, is barbarously killed and buried, unresisting, and rises again in golden beauty to save and renew his people's life. Interwoven with this legend is the idea of the blood-sacrifice with which you buy yourself off from the consequence of your own wrong-doing. Divine parentage was commonly attributed to kingly persons. Shaw did not believe that Jesus was divine. (Two Protestant sects of the nineteenth century had already put forward this view and still hold it.) He maintained that Jesus was simply an inspired leader and preacher who came to believe, himself, that he was the Messiah awaited by the Jews.

## The Gospels Without Prejudice

Shaw sets out to examine the gospels "without prejudice". Half a century later, his study of them is less startling than it was when he wrote it, simply because, since then, so many people have read and discussed his ideas. But he was the first writer to strip the conventional sanctimoniousness off the gospel story and look at it as if it was new. He pointed out that if you reject Christianity altogether you simply get classified as a heathen or a freethinker, quite placidly. But if you speak or write of Jesus Christ as a real live person, "If you venture to wonder how Christ would have looked if he had shaved or had his hair cut, or what size in shoes he took, or whether he swore when he stood on a nail in the carpenter's shop or could not button his robe in a hurry, or whether he laughed over the repartees by which he baffled the priests"—then the pious are as horrified and dismayed as Don Juan was when the statue stepped off its pedestal and came to supper with him. They are alarmed, because you have made the imaginary portrait become real. They have never thought of Christ as a real person who meant what he said, as a fact, as a force like electricity.

Each of the four evangelists, Shaw suggests, like all biographers, identifies the opinions and prejudices of his hero with his own personal ones. Matthew describes Jesus as a simple, downright preacher, a Bohemian, a stern peremptory disciple of John the Baptist, who never

addresses a Scribe or Pharisee without an insulting
epithet. Luke, who was himself an urbane person, sees
Jesus as gentle and sociable. In John's account he is an
educated, sophisticated mystic. But Shaw is not concerned
with the old wrangles about whether or not the gospels
are credible as matter-of-fact narratives. Belief is not
dependent on evidence or reason. It is a subjective state,
depending a great deal on the current fashion of one's day.
In the Middle Ages, people used to argue as to how many
angels could stand on the point of a pin. Today they argue
about how many million streptococci are contained in a
given volume of serum. Between the rejection of the
gospels as fabulous and complete acceptance of them there
will always be many different shades of belief and disbelief.
What interested Shaw was whether, if you threw away all
the miraculous part of Christianity there would be anything left of the mission of Jesus. "I am no more a
Christian than Pilate was, or you, gentle reader; and yet,
like Pilate, I greatly prefer Jesus to Annas and Caiaphas:
and I am ready to admit that after contemplating the
world and human nature for nearly sixty years, I see no
way out of the world's misery but the way which would
have been found by Christ's will if he had undertaken the
work of a modern practical statesman."

Shaw summed up some of the doctrines put forward by
Christ, as he saw them, from his own lifelong study of the
New Testament. (At Ayot St. Lawrence, in his study,
there is a Bible, marked "My travelling Bible" worn
white at the edges from much handling.) "God is a spirit
to be worshipped in spirit and truth and not an elderly
gentleman to be bribed or begged from." "Get rid of
your property by throwing it into the common stock."

"If you let a child starve, you are letting God starve."
"Get rid of judges and punishment and revenge." "Get
rid of your family entanglements. Every mother you meet
is as much your mother as the woman who bore you.
Every man you meet is as much your brother as the man
she bore after you."

Shaw believed that after Jesus was dead His followers
dragged down His authentic views to their own level, and
that is the level at which Christianity has remained ever
since. He thought that whereas Jesus had redeemed men
from folly and error, the apostles pulled them back into
their own prejudices, by reviewing old controversies and
performing vindictive miracles. They were joined by
Paul, whom Shaw visualized as an inhibited revivalist
preacher, who liked working up his audiences to hysteria
by describing his own conversion (and his misdeeds before
it) with great zest. Paul did not give up either his Roman
citizenship or his Judaism when he joined the movement,
but, said Shaw, added Judaism to his idea of what Jesus
had meant and called the result Christianity. Once Paul
took over the leadership, the programme of Jesus never
had a chance to get established, politically and socially.
Instead it was easily suppressed by the police while
Paulinism overran the whole civilized world.

### Established Religions

In *Androcles and the Lion* Shaw put forward the case for
the nonconformer who must rebel against the conventional
religion of his time and the freethinker who is really
searching for God. But eleven years later, in 1923, he had
developed his own philosophy further. In *Saint Joan* he
puts the case both for the nonconformer and for the sup-

porters of an established religion. Some kind of an established faith, he had come to believe, was necessary if men were to progress and become enlightened through it. Even Methodism (a faith he disliked because of its emphasis on the Atonement) had, through the Revivals, changed colliers and their wives and mothers from savages into civilized human beings. The play *Saint Joan* describes the clash between a saint and mystic who sees further than the conventional religious authority, and the authority which is obliged to destroy her because she is such a threat to the established faith. Shaw's Inquisitor and his Bishop are both just and merciful men. But they are dedicated to stamping out heresy, as a modern state has to stamp out typhus, before it spreads and destroys innocent people. During Joan's trial the monk who is acting as her defence counsel pleads that there is no real harm in her.

THE INQUISITOR (*dropping his blandness and speaking very gravely*). Brother Martin, if you had seen what I have seen of heresy, you would not think it a light thing even in its most apparently harmless and even lovable and pious origins.

He goes on to describe what develops when a saintly simpleton such as Joan defies social conventions and the rules of established religion.

The woman who quarrels with her clothes and puts on the dress of a man, is like the man who throws off his fur gown and dresses like John the Baptist; they are followed, as surely as the night follows the day, by bands of wild women and men who refuse to wear any clothes at all.

Shaw's conclusion is that although an established religion, like any other social organization, is bound to persecute nonconformers to some extent, it must all the same be able to adapt itself to change. A church which has no place for freethinkers turns its back on the law of God, which is the law of change, or evolution. If a church cannot believe that thought, when really free, must inevitably lead the freethinker to believe the church doctrines then it has no real faith in their truth itself.

## Science or Religion

Shaw was born at a time when the conventional church was tightening up its formulas against the attacks on accepted beliefs—not only Darwinism but the various rebel sects of the nineteenth century. He died before the churches themselves began to reform their doctrines, a hundred years later. Most reformers are promptly labelled atheists by those who would rather be left in the comfortable security of tradition than search for what they believe to be the real truth. Shaw was most bitterly attacked in his lifetime. But the biographers who knew him best describe him as a profoundly religious man. He said of his own search for truth, "There is nothing that people will not believe nowadays if only it be presented to them as science and nothing they will not disbelieve if it be presented to them as religion. I myself began like that and I am ending by receiving every scientific statement with dour suspicion, whilst giving very respectful consideration to the inspiration and revelation of the prophets and poets."

# 3   About Sex and Marriage

Shaw said, "I valued sexual experience because of its power of producing a celestial flood of emotion and exaltation which, however momentary, gave me a sample of the ecstasy that may one day be the normal condition of conscious intellectual activity."

*Sex*

He was "a continent virgin" until he was twenty-nine and married when he was forty-two, after which he had no more sexual adventures. In the years between he had many. He was a bachelor in a self-consciously Bohemian society and extremely attractive to women. "I was entirely free from the neurosis (as I class it) of Original Sin. I never associated sexual intercourse with delinquency." His only scruples were against buying sex, getting a woman into trouble or breaking up a marriage.

As the philanderer in *Getting Married* says, "Neither shall I be able to steal George's wife. I have stretched out my hand for that forbidden fruit before and I know that my hand will always come back empty. To disbelieve in marriage is easy: to love a married woman is easy; but to betray a comrade, to be disloyal to a host, to break the covenant of bread and salt is impossible."

He refused to consider sex as the most important thing in life. He never broke an engagement to speak on Socialism in order to spend a gallant evening. The romance which surrounded sexual love—the art and music and literature which it inspires—were, to him, far more interesting than the consummation. It was the love-affairs which were never consummated that he remembered in after years—his romance with Ellen Terry, conducted entirely through the post, and his tempestuous scenes with Mrs. Patrick Campbell, the other famous star for whom he wrote some of his most brilliant parts. Romances or "mystical betrothals"—which gave him inspirations for a play, or produced a set of letters which were a kind of literature in themselves—were valuable in a way that a brief sexual experience never could be. "What people call love is impossible except as a joke (and even then one of the two is sure to turn serious) between two strangers meeting accidentally at an inn or in a forest path." Romance was a luxury, a part of art—the "Uranian Venus". But marriage was the everyday stuff of life. In *The Apple-Cart*, Orinthia, King Magnus's "romantic affinity", is a recognizable portrait of Mrs. Patrick Campbell. She tells Magnus, haughtily, that he ought to divorce his common housekeeper wife and marry her.

ORINTHIA. What you need to make you a real king is a real queen.

MAGNUS. But I have got one.

ORINTHIA. Oh, you are blind. You are worse than blind: you have low tastes. Heaven is offering you a rose; and you cling to a cabbage.

MAGNUS (*laughing*). That is a very apt metaphor, beloved. But what wise man, if you force him to choose between doing without roses and doing without cabbages would not secure the cabbages?

## Prostitution

The first time Shaw came up against the Censor was over his play about prostitution, *Mrs Warren's Profession*. It was not because the subject itself was forbidden. Victorian literature is peppered with prostitute characters. But they are always described in a particular way, in a special tone of voice—a mixture of self-conscious charity and solemn rebuke. Shaw, on the contrary, was harshly unsentimental. His Mrs Warren is unrepentant. She would do the same thing again if she had her time over again. She had to do it because it was the only way she could make a good enough living to retain her self-respect. This was her defence. Her two half-sisters had been respectable girls.

MRS WARREN. Well, what did they get by their respectability? I'll tell you. One of them worked in a whitelead factory twelve hours a day for nine shillings a week until she died of lead poisoning. She only expected to get her hands a little paralyzed: but she died. The other was always held up to us as a model because she married a Government labourer in the Deptford victualling-yard and kept his room and the three children neat and tidy on eighteen shillings a week—

until he took to drink. That was worth being respectable for, wasnt it?

Shaw was not interested in apportioning guilt for Mrs Warren's way of making a living, but in the social system which made it necessary. The most quoted speech from this play has always been her summing-up of the economics of sex and marriage. "The only way for a woman to provide for herself decently is for her to be good to some man that can afford to be good to her." There was no real difference, she pointed out, between the Society lady who sets out to catch a rich husband for her daughter and the woman who offers a girl the chance to make a good living in one of her well-run "houses". "The house in Brussels was real high class: a much better place for a woman to be in than that factory where Anne Jane got poisoned." It was the firm belief of the early Fabians that once you rationalized the economics of employment, and gave every girl a chance to make a good living in reasonable conditions, no one would choose prostitution instead of ordinary work. The Fabians were regarded as impractical idealists; but, in fact, most of their beliefs about economic security and its effects have been justified. This one is the exception.

## Free Love

The intellectual rebels of the nineties were determined that the institution of conventional marriage must be reformed. Some of them liked to set an example by practising Free Love. It had to be done openly otherwise the gesture was wasted. The lovers used to move into a shared home and then send cards around to their friends announcing what they had done. Shaw disapproved. He himself was a most passionate supporter of marriage reform. But he did not think that private anarchical action was the way to it. "Young women come to me and ask me whether I think they ought to consent to marry the man they have decided to live with and they are perplexed and astonished when I who am supposed (heaven knows why!) to have the most advanced views on the subject urge them on no account to compromise themselves without the security of an authentic wedding-ring." One of his woman friends was most anxious to fix up this kind of union with him. She drew up an agreement about the terms of their relationship which they were both to sign, instead of a marriage contract. Shaw read it and was horrified. "Good God! This is worse than all the vows of all the churches on earth. I had rather be legally married to you ten times over."

## Marriage

It was the way sex was practised inside marriage which Shaw found far more shocking than extra-marital sex. As the hero of *Man and Superman* puts it, "Marriage is popular because it combines the maximum of temptation with the maximum of opportunity." Shaw was disgusted with the sexual slavery which is taken for granted by the most conventional couple. After a conference on marriage, composed of respectable married men, he reported: "They regarded the marriage ceremony as a rite which absolved them from the laws of health and temperance, inaugurated a lifelong honeymoon and placed their pleasures on exactly the same footing as their prayers. It seemed entirely proper and natural to them that out of every twenty-four hours of their lives they should pass eight shut up in one room with their wives alone and this not birdlike for the mating season but all the year round and every year."

His objection to the established tradition of marriage was that it was monstrously and immorally possessive. It disgusted him to hear a group of wives agreeing that they could never tolerate lending their husbands to another woman any more than they would lend their toothbrush.

He disliked the sentimental conception of an ideal home, "a family stewing in love from the cradle to the grave". In *Candida*, the Christian-Socialist parson describes his own perfect marriage to his curate. "Ah, my boy, get married: get married to a good woman; and then you'll understand. Thats a foretaste of what will be best in the Kingdom of Heaven we are trying to establish on earth." The curate is impressed; the parson's secretary is not.

LEXY. What a good man! What a thorough loving soul he is!

PROSERPINE (*impatiently*). Oh, a man ought to be able to be fond of his wife without making a fool of himself about her.

*Candida* was Shaw's version of Ibsen's theme of *A Doll's House*, the reality beneath the popular conception of the ideal marriage. Ibsen's hero was so much taken up with his own pose as a father-protector figure that he made a doll of his wife. Shaw's husband also poses as the strong man. But Candida is not a doll. She is so much the dominant partner that she can afford to let him play at being master. She says, "I build a castle of comfort and indulgence and love for him, and stand sentinel always to keep little vulgar cares out. I make him master here, though he does not know it and could not tell you a moment ago how it came to be so."

Shaw's most important and original philosophy about sex and marriage was that its "stern biological purpose" involved the woman pursuing the man, because she must have children. In *Man and Superman* this chase is recounted gaily and lightly, but Shaw was in earnest about it. He always put his most serious thought across to an audience through laughter. Halfway through the play, Tanner, the hero, realizes what is happening when his Cockney chauffeur tells that the young lady means to get him.

STRAKER. Ex-cuse me, you know, Mr. Tanner. But you asked me as man to man: and I told you as man to man.

TANNER (*wildly appealing to the heavens*). Then I—*I* am the bee, the spider, the marked-down victim, the destined prey.

STRAKER. I dunno about the bee and the spider. But the marked-down victim, thats what you are and no mistake: and a jolly good job for you, too, I should say.

When he is finally caught, Tanner accepts his destiny, but refuses to accept the romantic idea of a wedding as a cause for joy and congratulation.

TANNER. What we have both done this afternoon is to renounce happiness, renounce freedom, renounce tranquillity, above all renounce the romantic possibilities of an unknown future, for the cares of a household and family. I beg that no man may seize the occasion to get half-drunk and utter imbecile speeches and coarse pleasantries at my expense. We propose to furnish our own house according to our own taste; and I hereby give notice that the seven or eight travelling clocks, the four or five dressing-cases, the carvers and fish-slices, the copies of Patmore's Angel in the House in extra morocco, and the other articles you are preparing to heap upon us will be instantly sold and the proceeds devoted to circulating free copies of the Revolutionist's Handbook.

Shaw wrote *Getting Married* as a deliberate illustration of his views on the subject, at a time when his plays were produced as fast as he could write them. It was never a great success, perhaps because the plot is so obviously built up to cover definite aspects of the subject, and so it seems contrived, compared with both earlier and later plays. The points he deals with, in turn, are the English marriage laws; the economic dependence of the parties; the need for simplified divorce and the fact that there are plenty of other absorbing relationships between men and women apart from the consummation of sex. He believes that no self-respect between husband and wife is possible while one supports the other financially. (Jesus, he said, perceived that nobody could live the higher life unless money and sexual love were obtainable without sacrificing it, because a married man would try to please his wife and a married woman her husband instead of doing the work of God.) As marriage stands at present, a woman cannot free herself from an intolerable union without losing her livelihood into the bargain. She cannot go to the labour exchange and register herself as a wife and mother out of a job.

## Divorce

If the object of marriage is bliss, as the sentimentalists believe, then the very strongest reason for dissolving one must be that it is disagreeable to both parties. As Don Juan in Hell complains, in *Man and Superman*, "Those who talk most about the blessings of marriage and the constancy of its vows are the very people who declare that if the chain were broken and the prisoners left free to choose, the whole social fabric would fly asunder. You cannot have the argument both ways. If the prisoner is happy, why lock him in? If he is not, why pretend that he is?"

In modern marriage you start, said Shaw, by making an impossible promise. The marriage service insists that when two people are under the influence of the most violent and also the most transient of passions they must swear that they will remain in that excited, abnormal and exhausting condition continuously until death do them part.

Free and dignified divorce, in Shaw's view, would not destroy the institution of marriage at all. On the contrary, it would maintain it. It would put married couples on good behaviour, and it would transform the whole atmosphere of married life because, "As no room feels like a prison when the door is left open, the removal of the sense of bondage would at once make it much happier than it is now. Also, if the door were always open, there would be no need to rush through it as there is now when it opens for one moment in a lifetime and may never open again."

Shaw was placidly happy in his own marriage, which had been embarked upon free from the economic and possessive-sexual reasons which he thought so degrading. Looking back on it in old age, he summed up. "Not until I was past 40 did I earn enough to marry without seeming to marry for money, nor my wife at the same age without suspicion of being driven by sex starvation. As man and wife we found a new relation in which sex had no part. It ended the old gallantries, flirtations and philanderings for both of us."

*Chastity*

Shaw shocked the public of his day by his liberalism about sex, and by his frankness in discussing it. The late Victorians and the Edwardians may have been privately promiscuous but they did not find the topic of sex itself as absorbing as the generations who came after them found it. The audience or readers of today are not likely to be shocked by Shaw's views about extra-marital sex and divorce. They are likely to be just as shocked by something which their predecessors took in their stride—that is by Shaw's firm belief that sex was neither the most important nor the most interesting part of living. Apart from its biological importance, he thought it a childish obsession. The Ancient in *Back to Methuselah* has outgrown it. She explains to the adolescent that it is merely one of the charming playthings which she will enjoy for a while. "The most amusing child's toy is another child." But the adolescents, cramming the pleasures of the flesh into four years, and getting them over, have far greater pleasures awaiting them. One of the young people is already beginning to grow out of youth.

THE ANCIENT. Signs of maturity. Soon you will give up all these toys and games and sweets.
THE YOUTH. What! And be as miserable as you?
THE ANCIENT. Infant: one moment of the ecstasy of life as we live it would strike you dead.

# 4  About Socialism

Poverty, says the armaments millionaire in Shaw's *Major Barbara*, is the worst of crimes.

UNDERSHAFT. All the other crimes are virtues beside it; all the other dishonors are chivalry itself by comparison. Poverty blights whole cities; spreads horrible pestilences; strikes dead the very souls of all who come within sight, sound or smell of it. What you call crime is nothing; a murder here and a theft there; a blow now and a curse then; what do they matter? they are only the accidents and illnesses of life; there are not fifty genuine professional criminals in London. But there are millions of poor people, abject people, dirty people ill fed, ill clothed people. They poison us morally and physically, they kill the happiness of society; they force us to do away with our own liberties and to organize unnatural cruelties for fear they should rise against us, and drag us down into their abyss.

*The Crime of Poverty*

In this play the millionaire's daughter is a major in the Salvation Army. She "saves" her converts by helping them, with food and warmth and lodging, by finding them jobs, making them feel they belong and by the cheerful music characteristic of the "Army". (Shaw highly approved of their slogan—"Why should the devil have all the best tunes?") Her father, who admires and loves her, wants to give a donation to her shelter, but Barbara refuses because it is tainted money. They strike a bargain —a kind of bet—that each will examine the other's way of reforming the poor and see if either can convert the other. Undershaft visits Barbara's shelter and sees her way of dealing with the pitiful outcasts who come to her. Then she visits his armaments factory. She finds well-paid, self-respecting men, able to support their families properly, living in a model village, running their own co-operative insurance funds, pensions schemes and building society. They are not humble and grateful, as her converts are to her. On the contrary they disrespect-fully refer to their employer as Dandy Andy and consider him a cunning old rascal. Undershaft tells Barbara that if she brings the latest ruffian whose soul she is trying to save to work for him, he will convert him by giving him a good wage, a house and a permanent job. In a few months, says Undershaft, he will be a pillar of society.

BARBARA. And will he be the better for that?
UNDERSHAFT. You know he will. Dont be a hypocrite, Barbara. He will be better fed, better housed, better clothed, better behaved; and his children will be pounds heavier and bigger. That will be better than an American

cloth mattress in a shelter, chopping firewood, eating bread and treacle, and being forced to kneel down from time to time to thank heaven for it; knee drill, I think you call it. It is cheap work, converting starving men with a Bible in one hand and a slice of bread in the other. I will undertake to convert West Ham to Mahometanism on the same terms.

The happy ending—or tragedy—of this play is that Barbara has to confess herself defeated. "I cant talk religion to a man with bodily hunger in his eyes." She agrees to leave her outcasts, who sob with gratitude for a scrap of bread and treacle, and take on the well-paid factory-workers, fullfed, quarrelsome and uppish as they are, because that is where salvation is needed. Her father will never again be able to taunt her that her converts were bribed with bread.

Shaw used to say acidly that people supposed that because he was a Socialist he must love the poor. On the contrary he disliked them profoundly and had done ever since he was a child. He despised the genteel poverty of his own Downstart class, but he hated the squalor of the slum-life most of all. His nursemaid used to take him into the Dublin slums, so that she could visit her friends, when his parents believed he was being taken for an airing in the park. Seeing the slum-people did not inspire him with pity, but with a desire to eliminate them by making them comfortably off. In 1937, at the centenary of the Tolpuddle martyrs, he was asked to write the introduction to a book about them. He answered that he had no use for people who tried to alleviate poverty because if it was made bearable it would be borne instead of abolished.

*Equal Incomes*

His study of economics—he claimed—was the backbone of his plays, as much as the knowledge of anatomy was to the sculpture of Michelangelo. He explained his theories, with patience and charm, in *The Intelligent Woman's Guide to Socialism and Capitalism*. Political economy is the science of spending the national wealth in the most beneficial way. Wealth really consists of food which must be consumed soon after it is produced, and clothing which either wears out with use or perishes if it is not used. A nation, therefore, cannot divide up its wealth once and for all, but must divide it up every day and the question is on what basis it shall be shared out. Is it to be on the basis of every woman drawing what she had made by her own labour? The objection is that no one produces anything by herself except the woman who by her own painful, prolonged and risky labour produces a baby; and she cannot live on it. Instead it lives greedily on her. Is it to be divided on the basis of giving each what she deserves? Shaw gave an imaginary set of examination questions, assuming that virtue was the test of income. "Taking the money value of Jesus Christ as 100 and of Judas Iscariot as zero, give the correct figures for, respectively, Pontius Pilate, the proprietor of the Gadarene swine, the widow who put her mite in the poor-box, Mr. Horatio Bottomley, Shakespeare, Mr. Jack Johnson, Sir Isaac Newton, Palestrina, Offenbach, Sir Thomas Lipton, Mr. Paul Cinquevall, your family doctor." The third possibility is to let everyone have what she can lay her hands on, but this ends in robbery and violence. The fourth is the system already in use, by which about one person in ten is able to be rich without working, while the other nine work hard and long and are allowed just enough to keep them alive. The fifth is to divide it up by class so that dustmen and scavengers and rag-pickers should receive less for their work than teachers and opera-singers, and that judges and prime ministers should receive more. This is not, as you might think, the scheme we have at present, because those who exercise personal authority among us are by no means the richest people. Millionaires obey policemen. The captain of a liner has absolute authority over people who could afford to throw his pay into the sea and never miss it. The sixth possibility is to leave things as they are. But *laissez-faire* never results in things staying the same, because conditions change and get worse. The only solution, says Shaw finally, is to give everyone the same—the Socialist method of distributing wealth.

He believed that Communism was the plan of Christ's apostles and their followers. "Among them everybody threw all that she or he had into a common stock; and each took from it what he or she needed. The obligation to do this was so sacred that when Ananias and Sapphira kept back something for themselves, St. Peter struck them dead for 'lying to the Holy Ghost'."

*Leisure*

In the end, distribution of wealth simply means the distribution of leisure. At the time Shaw was writing he could claim with some justice that the invention of machinery had not resulted in any new distribution of leisure. In spite of the leisure created by machines, the population was still divided into the few who had the whole day free and the many who had barely four hours to dispose of as they pleased. He foresaw not only the

shorter working week of today, but a future in which
every person gave to the nation so many years of work,
and received, in return, his ration of so many years'
leisure. In *Back to Methuselah* Shaw pictures Britain in the
year 2170. By now everyone takes this system for granted.

But the Accountant-General of Britain discovers that
the Archbishop of Canterbury is secretly a Longliver. He
has already survived for two hundred and eighty-three
years. He has had to keep the fact quiet, however,
because ordinary short-lived people would have thought
of him as a monster, and probably killed him. So he
has pretended to die by drowning, several times over, and
returned to the world under a false name and taken a new
job. The Accountant-General, when he discovers this
deception, accuses the Archbishop of robbing the Exche-
quer, by drawing five or six incomes in his lifetime from
the State, when he was morally entitled to one only. But
oddly enough, Treasury accounts show a surplus not a
loss. He calls in the permanent head of the Civil Service,
a Chinaman named Confucius, to explain the disparity to
him. Confucius reminds him that in these days of an
enlightened Socialist economy, everyone starts work at
thirteen and retires at forty-three.

CONFUCIUS. That is, they do thirty years' work; and they
receive maintenance and education, without working,
for thirteen years of childhood and thirty-five years of
superannuation, forty-eight years in all, for each thirty
years' work. The Archbishop has given you 260 years'
work and has received only one education and no
superannuation. You therefore owe him over 300 years
of leisure and nearly eight educations. You are thus
heavily in his debt. In other words, he has effected an

enormous national economy by living so long; and you, by living only seventy-eight years, are profiting at his expense. He is the benefactor; you are the thief. (*Half rising*) May I now withdraw and return to my serious business, as my own span is comparatively short?

### Breakages Limited

The Fabians, whose economic policy was expressed by Shaw, believed in "the inevitability of gradualness", that is they believed in evolutionary socialism, in which the state would gradually take over responsibilities; not in nationalizing everything through a revolution. This means that some concerns would continue to be run by private enterprise, trading with the state. Shaw foresaw that such concerns would create vested interests and monopolies, and in *The Apple-Cart*, which he wrote in 1929, describes a future time when this has happened. In the play, Britain has been prosperous and contented for so long that the electorate has come to take this state of affairs completely for granted. At a Cabinet meeting one of the ministers comments that the voters are not interested in politics any longer.

BALBUS. Wages are too high, if you ask me. Anybody can earn from five to twenty pounds a week now, and a big dole when there is no job for him. And what Englishman will give his mind to politics so long as he can afford to keep a motor car?
NICOBAR. How many voted at the last election? Not seven per cent of the register.

By now the country has achieved prosperity for all by leaving the management of vital industries to big business men, who keep the constituents quiet by high wages; and real power is vested in the mammoth corporations. One of them, called Breakages Limited, which does every kind of repair, now has a monopoly of all repairs. Every breakdown, every smash and crash, is a job for them. This means that it is worth their while to buy up every invention of unbreakable and imperishable material and suppress it. One of the two women in the Cabinet, Lysistrata, the Powermistress Royal, finds that she cannot run the nation's motor power for the best benefit of the country as she should because Breakages Limited is able to harass and prevent her and she cannot stop them.

LYSISTRATA. They would set their private police to watch me day and night to get something against my private character. One of their directors told me to my face that by lifting up his finger he could get my windows broken by the mob; and that Breakages Limited would get the job of putting in new glass.

## Rich Socialist

Shaw himself was a very rich man for the second half of his life. His housekeeper said of him, "He was always complaining about the Government taking so much of his earnings in income tax and I often wondered if he was a Socialist at heart." She was not the only one to wonder. When Shaw's will was published, and it was revealed how rich he had been, there was a good deal of acid comment about the difference between theory and practice. But he had always persisted that it was the economics of Socialism and not the heroics which had first converted him and that if ever the system was thoroughly overhauled, and the national wealth divided up into equal shares for all, he would be perfectly satisfied with his share of it. Meanwhile he considered there was no point in getting rid of his own money for the sake of making an empty gesture. Giving away his own fortune might have been "an independent explosion of personal righteousness" but it would not have made any long-term difference to the system. His mission in life as he saw it was to write, preach, lecture and explain the way it should be reformed. He did this without minding whether he was paid for it or not. He never took a fee as a Socialist lecturer. He wrote his treatise *The Intelligent Woman's Guide to Socialism and Capitalism* at a period of his life when, if he had written another play instead, he could have made far more money in the time.

His pictures of the way poverty degrades a human being lasted on, immortal, long after reforms which he had urged had become the commonplace currency of everyday life. His portrait of the brothel-keeper, Mrs Warren, forced into taking it up because it was the only way an untrained woman could make a good living, still seems real and vivid, even in the days of full employment. The doctors he portrayed in *The Doctor's Dilemma*, unable to do their job properly because they were paid by private patients' fees, are still remembered, in the second decade of the National Health Service. Only the belief—which he shared with the Webbs—that once national poverty was eliminated crime and immorality would vanish with it is beginning to look a little faded. The kind of poverty which Shaw described in *Major Barbara* has almost disappeared. But Shaw did not live to see the Affluent Society which was established during the ten years after his death. It put his idea that economic security would automatically bring Utopia with it to the acid test.

# 5   About Democracy

*Law and Order*

" I was marching in a procession which numbered at least a thousand men. It was broken up and scattered in hopeless confusion and terror by twenty pale nervous policemen armed with nothing more deadly than their clubs." Shaw wrote this fifty years after the occasion, which was "Bloody Sunday" in November 1887. Some of the Fabians were marching with a rally of unemployed to Trafalgar Square. The contingent from Clerkenwell Green was broken up by police in High Holborn but some, including Shaw, made their way separately to Whitehall where they found that the police had already broken up the southern contingent. The rally was a complete failure. During the next week some of its leaders tried to whip up enthusiasm for another effort the following Sunday. Shaw poured cold water on the idea. He said that unless they could build barricades and were prepared to face machine-guns it was useless. "Since Bloody Sunday," Shaw confessed, "I have nothing but a sardonic smile for Shelley's 'Ye are many—they are few'."

This incident made a tremendous impression on Shaw. It shook his faith in a number of things in which he had believed unquestioningly. As an Irishman, he had been born and bred to see rebellion against tyranny as the first duty of a self-respecting man. As a young intellectual rebel he had seen himself as a leader of the underprivileged masses. It was easy for him to dominate a meeting as a speaker. But now, when it came to action, he found himself helpless. "One elderly man who recognized me as one of the orators who had exhorted the thousand to march to victory before the procession started, rushed up to me and cried, 'Tell us what to do. Give us a lead,' making me acutely conscious of my disgraceful exposure as an impotent windbag." This was the moment in his life when he turned away from the ideal of democratic government towards that of benevolent dictatorship, which he held until he died. "It made an end for me of the democratic delusion that the world is or ever can be ruled by majorities of unorganized individuals."

*Elected Governments*
He still insisted that he believed in "democracy", but he had his own interpretation of it. His definition was—"the organization of society for the benefit and at the expense of everyone indiscriminately". This is not exactly the interpretation of the western world today, which usually takes it to mean the rule of a government elected by universal adult suffrage. Shaw came to believe more and

more as he grew older that the ideal democracy would not necessarily include either the freedom to elect its government in the British way or personal liberty of the kind the British are used to. He always prophesied that a Marxist government once in power would in fact be much more reactionary than the capitalistic liberal democracies it had superseded. To him a bad government was simply a weak government. A strong one was a good one, even if it was tyrannical. He preferred tyranny to a policy of *laissez-faire*. The hallmark of a bad government was to be lazy or too timid to rule. Elected governments, he decided, were necessarily afraid to rule firmly and so could never be good governments. In his political play *The Apple-Cart*, Magnus, the philosopher-king, comments, "The people have found out long ago that democracy is humbug and that instead of establishing responsible government it has abolished it." The Trades Union leader (who owes his position in the Cabinet to an ordinary democratic election) remonstrates that he cannot sit there and hear such a word as humbug being applied to democracy. The king courteously apologizes. "You are right, Mr. Boanerges, as you always are. Democracy is a very real thing, with much less humbug about it than many older institutions. But it means, not that the people govern, but that the responsibility and the veto now belong neither to kings nor demagogues as such but to whoever is clever enough to get them."

In a broadcast in 1929 Shaw summed up his definition of true democratic government. He said that it was government of the people for the people, but not by the people. This last could never be a reality because the people could no more make their own laws than they could write their own plays. Both had to be done by professionals. Therefore the people are, in fact, always at the mercy of those who can govern.

The usefulness of suffrage, of having elections at all, in Shaw's view, is to prevent the people being entirely at the mercy of these professional governors. There were of course other ways of defying them. If the qualified governors oppress the people intolerably the people may be driven to burn their houses and tear them to pieces. But this is not only a clumsy solution, but an impractical one because autocrats are always tremendously popular with mobs. Autocrats, however, must not be left as they are, unchecked, simply because an absolute monarch or an absolute dictator almost always goes mad eventually. The conclusion is that the people must be able to change their governors by a legal arrangement when they do not suit. But this is not to say that the parliamentary system of today should remain. As Shaw saw the system of parliamentary democracy, it gave the electors the chance to choose only between one windbag and nincompoop and another. There should be no amateurs in government and therefore no amateurs among parliamentary candidates.

His plan was to have a group of the population as professional governors, trained and qualified for the job. He visualized that there should be several different levels of these qualified people. They would be classified into "panels". For instance, at the lower end of the scale there would be a panel of people qualified to take part in a parish meeting. Only the top panel would have those sufficiently well-qualified to act as Secretaries of State. Shaw considered that there might be only 2,000 people in Britain capable of taking their places on the highest panel, but that would be quite sufficient to give the electorate a choice of persons among the experts offered to them.

### Party Government

Besides his objection to politicians being unqualified amateurs, Shaw objected to their being divided into parties. He hated and despised the whole party-government system. *In Everybody's Political What's What*, he explains by illustrating in a dramatic sketch the reason why the party system first began in Britain. This short play of his is founded on historical fact. In 1690, the king, William III, was advised by Robert Spencer, the Earl of Sunderland, to choose all his ministers from one party. Shaw sees this incident as the origin of the modern Cabinet.

ROBERT. I have a scheme for dealing with Parliament though I have never yet found a king subtle enough to understand it.

WILLIAM. Try me.

ROBERT. You, sire, are the last king on earth to understand it. But I will lay it at your royal feet. Just now you choose your ministers on their merits and capacities without regard to their parties, a Whig here a Tory there, each in his department which you call his Cabinet and the assembly of them forming your council which may be called *your* Cabinet.

WILLIAM. Just so. What fault have you to find with that?

ROBERT. My advice to your Majesty is that in future you shall choose all your ministers from the same party and that this party shall always be the party which has a majority in the House of Commons.

WILLIAM. You are mad. Whoever heard of such a thing?

Robert explains that once his plan is established, no
M.P. will ever again vote according to his principles or
his convictions or his judgment or his religion, because he
will always really be voting on one issue alone—that is
whether or not his own party shall stay in power.

ROBERT. He will spend half his life and most of his means
in getting into Parliament and when at last he arrives
there he will have no time to think of anything but how
to get into your Majesty's Cabinet. When he intrigues
his way to the top of that, he will be a master of the
party game and of nothing else. He will feed out of your
Majesty's hand. And the people will imagine they are
free because they have a Parliament. Then you can fight
all Europe all the time to your heart's content.

Shaw's argument was that a parliament composed of
political parties was so hampered by the system that it
never could get anything done. In the two centuries of
the British parliament's deplorable existence it had not
approached the record of the Russian Soviet's first twenty
years of power. All the same, he did believe that parliamentary government, as such, should survive and continue to rule, but with the party system eliminated.
Parliament itself was necessary to freedom and progress
as "a congress of plaintive and plangent Anybodies, with
unlimited license to complain, to criticise, to denounce,
to demand, to suggest . . . in short to keep the government
abreast of public sentiment."

*Free Speech*
He also believed in untramelled Free Speech for everybody. The right to hold demonstrations and public

meetings must be jealously preserved. "The young men must have a platform to shout from, for a government must know what the young Calvins, Napoleons, Hitlers, and Ataturks have to say, and how far they are converting the public or being hissed by it. Without such contact the ruling sages may get dangerously out of touch with the spirit of the age."

In Shaw's play *On the Rocks* (which he wrote after he had visited Soviet Russia and been tremendously impressed by it) the hero is a democratic prime minister, so hampered by tradition that he is unable to govern. All he can do is to fall back on the policy of *laissez-faire* which Shaw despised so bitterly. Everything has gone wrong with Britain on account of it. Processions of unemployed are blocking all the streets and the Commissioner of Police is at his wits' end to find ways of keeping order. In the play, a veteran Trades Union Leader, Hipney, who started as a revolutionary Socialist, blames it all on the old parliamentary system.

HIPNEY. Adult suffrage; that was what was to save us all. My God! It delivered us into the hands of our spoilers and oppressors, bound hand and foot by our own folly and ignorance. It took the heart out of old Hipney; and now I'm for any Napoleon or Mussolini or Lenin or Chavender that has the stuff in him to take both the people and the spoilers and oppressors by the scruffs of their silly necks and just sling them into the way they should go.

Hipney thinks that the people are already governed by irresponsible little dictators, anyway; by the landlord who can turn you out of your house if you do not pay him for the right to exist on earth, and by the employers who can sack you if you stand up to them as a man and an equal. What he wants is for the people to have the right to choose their government, from alternatives composed only of qualified men. The people cannot sort out the capable from the incapable. This must be done for them first.

HIPNEY. How are they to tell the difference between any cheap Jack and Solomon or Moses? The Jews didnt elect Moses; he just told them what to do and they did it. Look at the way they went wrong the minute his back was turned!

Shaw's increasing contempt for democratic procedures, and for the politicians elected by the British system, turned many of his most serious disciples away from him. As he grew older he became more fixed in his ideas and less tolerant. His passion for a strong government led him to praise Hitler and Mussolini and Stalin, and to dismiss their tyrannies and cruelties as something that did not matter much, and would undoubtedly be reformed in time, as their systems of government settled down. The Shaw of the thirties was politically both less flexible and less inspiring than the Shaw of the nineties, who had composed the Fabian pamphlets. It is possible that the more remote he got from the everyday business of politics, the more hidebound he became within his own theories. Webb, whose career kept him in the down-to-earth world of practical politics, remained truer to the ideals they had worked out together as young men. It was perhaps the remoteness of Shaw from political work, and his absorption in theory which narrowed his thinking in this way.

The only actual administrative work he ever did was in local government; and his ideas about this remained liberal and flexible to the end.

*Local Government*

When he was an elected member of St. Pancras vestry, Shaw worked so hard and enthusiastically that he had a breakdown and was forced to give it up. St. Pancras honoured him by making him a Freeman of the borough and the certificate to that effect always had a place of honour in Shaw's house at Ayot St. Lawrence. He believed in local government, because it really got things done which affected the everyday lives of normal people. One of the Webbs' political inspirations was that there ought really to be two parliaments, one to decide the laws, and the other to concentrate on social questions. Shaw found the local council the nearest thing to a social parliament. He called it the "Parliament of the Poor". He and a young Methodist minister on the St. Pancras Vestry electrified the borough, trying to "push the rates up and keep the death-rate down". In the early nineteen-hundreds local government was free from the authority of party whips (unlike the present situation) and Shaw himself in pursuit of his idea of freedom from party commitment always tried to come to agreement with the other side, to the extent of arranging uncontested elections whenever possible. The idea of a committee of people whose opinions generally might differ widely, working out a line of procedure in the committee room and then defending it to the whole council and the public at large, was to him a far more satisfactory political method than cabinet government.

## World Government

In common with most political writers of his day he acknowledged that the world must have a supra-state constitution if it was to survive. The League of Nations was held back by the impossible condition that all its decisions should be unanimous. Shaw believed that the only hope for the future lay in such organizations as the International Court of Justice and the International Labour Office. In his play *Geneva*, which he was just finishing in 1939 (when international co-operation reached a new low) three dictators, Battler, Bombardone and Flanco (or Hitler, Mussolini and Franco) all turn up to answer the summons of individuals they have injured, at Geneva. They defend their own ideas and ideologies, but all discussion is stopped by the announcement that humanity is doomed. The earth has jumped in its orbit, and is now millions of miles further from the sun. So, within a few months, icecaps will have spread, the human race will not be able to survive and even the polar bears will be frozen stiff. In the circumstances, the democracy, the fascism, communism and catholicism which everyone has been arguing about all become completely meaningless. It was a favourite theory of Shaw's that only an elemental disaster could wipe out political-ideological differences between nations. In 1945—after the dropping of the atom bomb—he added a preface to this play about international co-operation. In it he said that perhaps the next great invention might be so terrible that "it may create an overwhelming interest in pacific civilization and wipe out war." Two decades later it still seems possible he was right.

# 6 About Crime and Punishment

Shaw said, "I have no special sympathy with the criminal in his cell. I am revolted by the cruelty of putting anyone in a cell. My alternative, which is to kill the criminal if he cannot be trusted at large, would not strike him as sympathetic."

*Revenge*
He did not believe in punishment of any kind, in any part of civilized life. Punishment is simply revenge, wrapped up in hypocrisy. It combines a chance to moralize with a chance to exercise the dark lust for cruelty which is a perversion of the sex instinct. He saw no basic difference between putting a criminal on the rack in the old way, and birching him on the order of a modern court of justice. Both consisted of "trumping up a moral case" against

him and then cold-bloodedly enjoying your vengeance. If people were too dangerous to be permitted to live, they must be quickly and painlessly put out of the way. He first illustrated this in *Caesar and Cleopatra*. Caesar is Shaw's picture of the most nearly-perfect leader and lawgiver of all time. In the play, Rufio, one of Caesar's officers, admits that he had killed Cleopatra's nurse because she was a treacherous and dangerous assassin.

CLEOPATRA (*vehemently*). He has shed the blood of my servant Ftatateeta. On your head be it as upon his, Caesar, if you hold him free of it.

CAESAR (*energetically*). On my head be it, then; for it was well done. Rufio; had you set yourself in the seat of the judge, and with hateful ceremonies and appeals to the gods handed that woman over to some hired executioner to be slain before the people in the name of justice, never would I have touched your hand without a shudder. But this was natural slaying; I feel no horror at it.

Shaw's views about crime and punishment are based on two ruling principles of his life from which he never deviated. The first is that cruelty is the worst evil in the whole of human life, the sin against the Holy Ghost, a part of human nature so obscene that he could hardly bear to contemplate it. The second is that the more civilized a community becomes, the more disciplined it must be, insisting on a certain standard of behaviour and service from all its members. It was the combination of these two beliefs which drove him into believing that anyone who could not reach the required standard must be painlessly exterminated. In *Back to Methuselah*, a pompous visitor to the country of the super-civilized Longlivers deliberately insults one, meaning to make her angry, which is a strange sensation for her, since the Longlivers have, ages since, outgrown the lust for violence.

Zoo. Something very disagreeable is happening to me. I feel hot all over. I have a horrible impulse to injure you. What have you done to me?

She begins to wonder whether a man who can have such an effect ought to be trusted at large.

Zoo. Whatever you are doing it is something so utterly evil that if you do not stop it I will kill you.
THE ELDERLY GENTLEMAN (*apprehending his danger*). Doubtless you think it safe to threaten an old man——
Zoo (*fiercely*). Old! you are a child: an evil child. We kill evil children here. We do it even against our own wills, by instinct. Take care.

Anything which deliberately imposed suffering upon another human being to Shaw was a part of revenge, not a part of this necessary removal of the unfit-for-society. Imprisonment was a deliberate imposition of suffering, and simply proved that the imprisoner was worse than the imprisoned. Joan of Arc chooses to be burnt alive rather than locked up for the rest of her life.

JOAN. You promised me life, but you lied (*indignant exclamations*). You think that life is nothing but not being stone dead. It is not bread and water I fear: I can live on bread; when have I asked for more? It is no hardship to drink water if the water be clean. Bread has no sorrow for me, and water no affliction. But to shut me from the light of the sky and the sight of the fields and flowers; to chain my feet so that I can never again ride with the soldiers or climb the hills; to make me breathe foul damp darkness, and keep me from everything that brings me back to the love of God when your wickedness and foolishness tempt me to hate Him; all this is worse than the furnace in the Bible that was heated seven times.

In 1947, when Parliament debated the abolition of the death penalty, Shaw wrote that he was in favour of retaining and extending it. He thought that those whom he classed as freaks—such as murderously violent men, women poisoners, vitriol-throwers and other essentially dangerous personalities—should be pitied, but painlessly killed, without malice, as a mad dog is killed. But his definition of unfit-to-live—ominously—did not stop at what we should call psychopathic cases. It extended to all who were not worth their salt and who were spoiling the lives of those who were worth their salt and a bit more. On the mantelpiece of his home at Ayot St. Lawrence the photograph of the Soviet commissar Djerjinsky shares the place of honour with those of Ghandi, Lenin, Stalin and Shaw's old friend and colleague Granville-Barker. Djerjinsky was responsible for the railways in the early years of the U.S.S.R. He found that his written instructions to the staff of a remote country station were being persistently ignored. He put a revolver in his pocket, travelled down to the station and shot the stationmaster. Shaw admired Djerjinsky for it. He commented, "Thus did he pick himself out as an executive officer by his readiness to pick other people off if they stood in the way of the transport which was the circulation of Russia's life-blood."

*Prison Reform*

Shaw impatiently dismissed the claims of those who believe that all criminals are capable of reform, saying that any who can be reformed are not really criminals and therefore do not come into the argument. But he differentiated between imprisoning a man in order to punish him (or take revenge on him) and putting him in a place of safety where he can be out of mischief. He pointed out that originally prisons were not intended as places of punishment at all, but as places where the offender was detained until punishment was decided on or until he paid what he owed. For instance, the Fleet prison, as described in Pickwick, was an establishment in which you could have the comforts of life—other than liberty—and where people could visit you. It was only later that prisons became penal institutions instead of places of safe-keeping. The first idea was better than the last. They should return to being communities in which those unable to keep up the civilized standards of life in the outside world should live in a small one specially planned to fit them. These prison communities—far from being made purposely disagreeable, as they are under our present system of retribution—should be as comfortable and happy as possible, because the people in them are simply being kept apart, as in an isolation hospital, not punished. Shaw visualized that they would come to prefer prison to the outside world because it would fit them better. Even if they were offered release, they would choose to stay on, as men who are discharged from the army and cannot cope with the responsibilities of making their own decisions, in civilian life, sign on for a further period of service. He quoted the example of a humanely conducted convict settlement he had seen in Soviet Russia, which had grown into a flourishing industrial concern because convicts chose to stay on in it after the expiration of their sentences.

## Trial by Jury

But the unfit-to-live have got to be sorted out from the reformable, and society has got to have some method of arrest and trial. Shaw favoured a system of his own invention which he admitted would take all Protestants aback: it was to revive the idea of the Roman Catholic court of the Inquisition, though it would be stripped, needless to say, of all the cruelties with which its name is associated. It would be a court of inquiry and it would come into the picture only *after* the anti-social person had been judged by the ordinary law.

The law, Shaw said, must be utterly inflexible and logical. But there must be, between the law and the citizen, some buffer, some institution which is flexible and human, which is moved by mercy and compassion, by respect for persons and consideration of circumstances and pressing political expediency. In British courts this really ought to be the function of the jury. There was no need for a jury to decide whether or not Tom had killed Dick. The police and the judge could decide that for themselves "without the interference of twelve pro-miscuous ratepayers". The real use of the jury ought to be to decide whether there was any excuse for Tom, on human grounds. They ought to be "an agent of grace" to stand between him and the inflexible law, as the sovereign's prerogative of mercy is today.

Shaw thought that his (non-punishing) Inquisition would be a better "agent of grace" than a jury. The police would bring the case, but the judge would not pass sentence. Instead he would report the verdict to this Inquisition which would decide whether the accused could safely be allowed to go on living. If not he would be found dead in his bed, having gone to sleep in perfect health, expecting to wake as usual.

When critics argued that if the state had this right to make secret decisions and secret exterminations, no one would ever be able to be certain, when he went to bed, of waking up next morning, Shaw retorted impatiently that this would be a good thing, because it would make the ordinary citizen more careful to be sure that he was pulling his weight for the common good. It would produce a sense of social responsibility which at the moment is actively discouraged.

### Negative Laws

It was discouraged, he said, by the fact that so-called democracy—by which he meant the present system of Parliamentary government—is only enthusiastic about negative laws. These are the laws which stand between the citizen and the power of the state such as Magna Carta, Habeas Corpus, trial by jury and freedom of speech. Any hint of positive legislation—by which the state regulates the life of the individual—sends the voters rushing to the polling station to vote against it. But the advance of civilization—which he equated with the coming of universal Socialism—must mean that the state interferes more and more in everyday life.

### Self-deception?

It is difficult to reconcile Shaw's theoretical callousness about individual life with his passionate pleading for mercy at all costs. He detested Pavlov, the Russian scientist, more than Nero because his experiments involved what Shaw called the obscene torturing of dogs. Shaw refused to believe that any knowledge gained by the experiments could justify the means. Beside this, his own icy belief in the extermination of the unfit seems illogical. But it is, in fact, rather his detestation of cruelty and his belief in state control pushed to the absurdity of their logical conclusion. In a regulated society something must be done about misfits. Shaw would rather have them put out of sight straight away than face up to seeing them manhandled. It was the subjective reaction of a sensitive and civilized man. But his weakness was, perhaps, that he tried to justify it rationally. He closed his eyes to what he could not bear to contemplate and then tried to make out a case that it was not there, as he did over the concentration camps. He once wrote that a possible explanation of the actions of the guards was that the government had failed to supply food for the prisoners and so they let them starve to death as the simplest solution. The housekeeper who was with him during his last years reported, "He could not bring himself to believe in the German concentration camps like Dachau and Belsen. He was so very clever, yet he was a simple man in some directions—unpractical and living in the skies like so many artists and thinkers are."

# 7 About War

"A cavalry charge! Think of that! He defied our Russian commanders—acted without orders—led a charge on his own responsibility—headed it himself—was the first man to sweep through their guns. Cant you see it, Raina: our gallant splendid Bulgarians, with their swords and eyes flashing, thundering down like an avalanche and scattering the wretched Serbs and their dandified Austrian officers like chaff. And you! you kept Sergius waiting a year before you would be betrothed to him. Oh, if you have a drop of Bulgarian blood in your veins you will worship him when he comes back."

This is the romantic view of war. It is one of the opening speeches of Shaw's first successful play, *Arms and the Man*. Later in the scene we get the other side of the picture, from a man who was actually in the battle.

THE MAN. You never saw a cavalry charge, did you?
RAINA. How could I?
THE MAN. Ah, perhaps not. No: of course not! Well, it's
a funny sight. It's like slinging a handful of peas against
a window pane: first one comes: then two or three close
behind him: and then all the rest in a lump.
RAINA (*her eyes dilating as she raises her clasped hands
ecstatically*). Yes, first One! the bravest of the brave.
THE MAN (*prosaically*). Hm! you should see the poor devil
pulling at his horse.
RAINA. Why should he pull at his horse?
THE MAN (*impatient of so stupid a question*). It's running
away with him, of course: do you suppose the fellow
wants to get there before the others and be killed? Then
they all come. You can tell the young ones by their
wildness and their slashing. The old ones come
bunched up under the number one guard: they know
that theyre mere projectiles and that it's no use trying
to fight. The wounds are mostly broken knees, from the
horses cannoning together.

*Anti-Romantic*
Shaw wrote this play to attack romantic idealism about
war. At the time he was writing, Britain had not been
involved in a full-scale one for thirty-eight years. Military
romanticism thrives in a long period of peace, when there
are no inconvenient maimed soldiers on the streets or
mourning households or national debts to cloud it. The
last—and the most fantastic ever—outbreak of romancing
had been over the charge of the Light Brigade in the
Crimean War. It had been the same kind of cavalry
charge as the one described in *Arms and the Man*. The
real-life one happened because of an official error. The
brigade was ordered to charge into a valley bristling with

guns, where they could only be slaughtered. They were slaughtered. Tennyson, who was Poet Laureate, wrote his poem about the charge to cover up the truth and present it as a glorious military saga, praising the soldiers who obeyed the fatal order without question. "Theirs not to reason why, Theirs but to do and die." In Shaw's play, he lightens the horror by making the enemy suffer a similar mistake on the part of their officers. They have been issued with the wrong-sized cartridges and so the charging cavalry win after all.

Tennyson's disguising of the brutal facts was exactly the kind of attitude which Shaw was attacking. The critics were shocked and indignant. So were audiences. Edward VII commented angrily, "Whoever the author is, he is, of course, mad." Today, seventy years and three wars later, it is difficult to appreciate just how important the romanticizing of militarism was to the British people then. It was the basic belief of the whole faith in the British Empire, by which Britain was specially appointed by God to rule one-fifth of the world. Ordinary people had their everyday lives coloured by feeling themselves a small part of this divine mission. The upper class family which had a son who was an officer in the service of the British Empire felt it most. But the working-class one with a private in the family shared it. Kipling's Tommy, dreaming of his period of service in Mandalay—

"And I'm learnin' 'ere in London wot the ten-year soldier tells,
If you've 'eard the East a-callin' you won't never 'eed naught else,"

represented something real in English life. Shaw's mockery of the tradition seemed a kind of blasphemy. To find a parallel today, you have to imagine what the reaction would be if a Soviet writer took to mocking the whole ideal of its cosmonauts.

In *Arms and the Man*, Shaw exposes what he calls the amateurism of the glory-hunting soldier, through the attitude of a Swiss mercenary, a professional, who is in the business, not for the sake of patriotism, but as a job. He is contemptuous of the cavalry officer who led his men, not only to certain death but to certain defeat. "Is it professional to throw a regiment of cavalry on a battery of machine-guns with the dead certainty that if the guns go off not a horse or a man will ever get within fifty yards of the fire?" When he discovers that he is talking to the fiancée of the officer in question he is apologetic.

THE MAN. Perhaps I'm quite wrong, you know: no doubt I am. Most likely he had got wind of the cartridge business somehow, and knew it was a safe job.
RAINA. That is to say he was a pretender and a coward! You did not dare say that before.
THE MAN (*with a comic gesture of despair*). It's no use, dear lady. I cant make you see it from the professional point of view.

Shaw's mercenary was not the conventional stage soldier. "He suffers from want of food and sleep: his nerves go to pieces after three days under fire, ending in the horrors of a rout and pursuit; he has found by experience that it is more important to have a few bits of chocolate to eat in the field than cartridges for his revolver." The impression which this prosaic detail alone made on the military-romanticists is shown by the fact that when the play was made into a musical comedy it was called "The Chocolate Soldier," from the quotation:

THE MAN. You can always tell an old soldier by the inside of his holsters and cartridge boxes. The young ones carry pistols and cartridges, the old ones, grub."

It was not difficult, Shaw told his critics, to prove that these unromantic facts were true. They had only to ask the nearest soldier. But it was not so much a matter of fact that was at issue as a whole way of thought. To the British public of the nineties, taking the romance out of war meant a denial of the existence of courage, patriotism and faith in the empire.

All practitioners of literature discover that it is fatally easy to concentrate on the colour and glamour of war, to wrap up barbarism in a disguise of chivalrous heroism. The wisest of French kings, Henry of Navarre, is remembered not for his aim that every French peasant should have a chicken in the pot but for the ballad about his white plume in the battle of Ivry. Shaw himself was not immune from this fascination. As a boy he had acted out battles and sword-fights when he came home from seeing them at the theatre. He had gloried in the thunder of captains and the shouting in the Bible and in the fight between Christian and Apollyon in *Pilgrim's Progress*. When he was invited to visit the Front, during the 1914 war, he was surprised and shocked to find himself exhilarated by the experience. "I am bound to state plainly as a simple fact, to be exploited by devils or angels according to its true nature, that I enjoyed myself enormously and continuously." The eeriness of the ruined landscape, the sound of the guns—"German music"—and the companionship of men who lived matter-of-factly close to death all the time, had a powerful effect on him. In *Heartbreak House* he described the effect of an air-raid on the characters. They are driven wild by excitement. "Did you hear the explosions? And the sound in the sky: it's splendid, it's like an orchestra: it's like Beethoven."

## Common-Sense

During the 1914 war, Shaw was classed as a pacifist, along with the "white-feather" non-combatants, traitors and "conchies"—with everyone who did not share in the patriotic fervour of the time. But he never was specifically a pacifist—that is one who believes that violence is wrong in itself. During the South African war, when everyone expected him to be anti-war, like the other Fabians, who looked on it as an imperialist campaign, he was, on the contrary, in favour of it. Ibsen, who at all other times was anti-British, had just announced that this time he was against the South Africans because they were a theocratic society (that is, taking their authority straight from the Old Testament) and perhaps Shaw thought that where Ibsen led he must follow. But when the 1914 war broke out, Shaw wrote a pamphlet, "Common-Sense About the War", which violently attacked the British for declaring it. He blamed the politicians, whose drifting policy had made it inevitable, but most of all the hypocrisy of Britain's crusading attitude. The British Navy, he said, had been preparing for this particular fight for years, just as the Germans had been waiting for *Der Tag*. Now Britain was posing as a sucking-dove of peace. He derided the

"Gallant Little Belgium" slogan, pointing out that all we were doing for the Belgian people, after all, was to use their land as a battle-field. Above all he abused the Christian churches for encouraging the nations to "pray to their common Father to assist them in sabring and bayoneting and blowing one another to pieces". Some British clergy were using their pulpits to whip up war fever and anti-German demonstrations. Shaw suggested that before doing so they should take off their cassocks and admit that they had now discovered that the Gospel of Peace which they had preached all these years was dangerous nonsense, instead of "serving Mars in the name of Christ to the scandal of all religious mankind".

## Terrible Joy

Before the war he had begun *Heartbreak House*, a picture of drifting, indecisive England, on the way to disaster. But in *Back to Methuselah* he aimed at studying the fundamental reasons why human beings are fascinated by war. In the garden of Eden, Cain is the first military man. Adam lives by digging; Abel by planning and inventing. He is a discoverer, a man of ideas. But Cain can only fulfil himself by destruction—by hunting animals and fighting men. He does not want to live for ever. He only wants to live bravely and die early and make room for others. Because of him, the life-span of all Eve's children will be shortened. He is the man who is in love with death instead of life.

The next episode of Shaw's play is set in the nineteen-twenties and Cain's successors have just made the greatest war in history so far. The old have survived; the young have had their lives shortened by the old men's "crusade".

It is this that makes the two scholars work out their theory that man must learn to live for three centuries instead of seventy years if the human race is to survive. In another episode, set in the future, the short-livers, who still die off early, are still in the hands of the military men. One of these, who is a re-incarnation of Napoleon, comes to consult the Longliver's oracle. His problem is that he is a military genius, and can only fulfil himself by organizing slaughter.

NAPOLEON. Now this great game of war, this playing with armies as other men play with bowls and skittles, is one which I must go on playing, partly because a man must do what he can and not what he would like to do, and partly because, if I stop, I immediately lose my power and become a beggar in the land where I now make men drunk with glory.

THE ORACLE. No doubt then you wish to know how to extricate yourself from this unfortunate position?

NAPOLEON. It is not generally considered unfortunate, madam. Supremely fortunate, rather.

He does not shed blood with his own hand. His talent is to provide for other people the "terrible joy they call glory". His armies die with shouts of triumph on their lips. But if he goes on exercising his genius, it will cost the world "the demoralization, the depopulation, the ruin of the victors no less than of the vanquished." He wants the oracle to advise him how he can go on fulfilling himself in the only way he can until he dies.

THE ORACLE. The way out of your difficulty is very simple.

NAPOLEON (*eagerly*). Good. What is it?

THE ORACLE. To die before the tide of glory turns. Allow me. (*She shoots him.*)

*Military Genius*

The real romantic attraction of war, to Shaw, was the military geniuses which it produced. Napoleon, Julius Caesar and Joan of Arc all fascinated him. Before he wrote *Caesar and Cleopatra*, he studied the histories of Caesar's strategy and tactics. At the beginning of the play a fugitive Egyptian soldier describes what it feels like to be up against Caesar's army.

BEL AFFRIS. But this Caesar does not pit man against man; he throws a legion at you where you are weakest as he throws a stone from a catapult: and that legion is as a man with one head, a thousand arms and no religion. I have fought against them. I know.

BELZANOR (*derisively*). Were you frightened, cousin?

*The guardsmen roar with laughter, their eyes sparkling at the wit of their captain.*

BEL AFFRIS. No, cousin, but I was beaten. They were frightened (perhaps); but they scattered us like chaff.

*The guardsmen, much damped, utter a growl of contemptuous disgust.*

There were two young men whose names have survived to become legends of the 1914 war. One was Rupert Brooke, who died at the beginning of it. He stood for all that Shaw most bitterly opposed. He was a poet who romanticized the Great War as Tennyson had the Crimean War, with his poems welcoming it as a crusade. "Now God be thanked Who has matched us with His hour," and "If I should die think only this of me." But the second legend—that of T. E. Lawrence who created the "Revolt in the Desert" which turned the tide for the

Allies in the middle east—was one which caught Shaw's imagination as much as all the stories of Caesar and Napoleon. Lawrence and Shaw were close friends, and when Lawrence wanted to hide from his own fame, he took Shaw's name, and used it instead of his own. Shaw had the deep respect for Lawrence which a stay-at-home writer sometimes develops for the successful man of action. He put a recognizable portrait of Lawrence into one of his later plays, *Too True to be Good*, called Private Meek. But *Saint Joan* which was written at the time when the story of Lawrence's exploits was at the height of its popularity is about a military genius who did much what Lawrence did. Joan, says Shaw, "lectured, talked down and overruled statesmen, pooh-poohed the plans of generals, leading their troops to victory on plans of her own. She had an unbounded and quite unconcealed contempt for official opinion, judgment and authority and for War Office tactics and strategy." If you replace Joan's name with that of Lawrence in the description it is still authentic history. Like Lawrence, Joan united a scattered and demoralized nation to turn the occupying invaders out of their country. Like Lawrence, she felt herself cast aside and deserted by her colleagues once the victory was won.

Joan's inspiration was to put a fighting spirit into the disunited and disillusioned French soldiers.

JOAN. You do not understand, squire. Our soldiers are always beaten because they are fighting only to save their skins; and the shortest way to save your skin is to run away. Our knights are thinking only of the money they will make in ransoms; it is not kill or be killed with them, but pay or be paid. But I will teach them all to fight that the will of God may be done in France and then they will drive the poor goddams before them like sheep.

In Joan's hour of triumph, she begins to realize that her supporters are anxious to get rid of her. Dunois, her comrade-in-arms, rallies her, in a speech which might have been addressed to Lawrence. Joan protests that the authorities are opposing her, though she has brought them luck and victory and set them right when they were doing stupid things.

JOAN. Then why do they not love me?
DUNOIS (*rallying her*). Sim-ple-ton! Do you expect stupid people to love you for showing them up? Do blundering old military dug-outs love the successful young captains who supersede them? Do ambitious politicians love the climbers who take the front seats from them?

Shaw sent Lawrence a copy of *Saint Joan* to read before it was produced. Lawrence wrote to Mrs. Shaw praising the play, particularly what he called "the fighting part". He added, "Take care, he may yet write an epic of bloodlust."

*1939*
He never did. But his growing admiration for the totalitarian states which grew up between the wars so coloured his judgment that he never accused their militarism of being a romanticized crusade. The prudent statesman, he decided, cannot do without the military man. "He must even provide for the special education of a certain proportion of the population as military men; that is as romantic barbarians." Impotent governments, with obsolete ideologies, however democratic they might be

in form, would always go down before up-to-date con-
querors. Shaw admired the dictators because they were
strong governments, not afraid to govern, and capable of
forcing social reform on their peoples. He was, in fact,
curiously ignorant about modern Europe and knew considerably less about it than Shakespeare knew about the
Europe of his day. He had visited Soviet Russia and been
extremely impressed by it, and from then on Stalin, in his
eyes, could do no wrong. A few weeks after the beginning
of the 1939 war, he wrote, about Stalin's move against
Poland, "Fortunately, our old pal Stalin stepped in at the
right moment and took Hitler by the scruff of the neck; a
masterstroke of foreign policy with six million red soldiers
at its back." A few weeks later, he wrote an article for the
*New Statesman* in which his first-war pamphlet had been
published, called, this time, "Uncommon Sense About
the War". In it he praised Stalin, and said that if it had
not been for our treatment of Germany after 1918, Hitler
would still have been a struggling artist of no account and
that instead of railing at our own creation we should
recognize the ability with which he had undone our wicked
work and make peace with him.

The tolerance with which Shaw's anti-war propaganda
was received in the second war, as compared with the
first, is the difference between the 1914 outlook and that
of 1939. This time there were no illusions for him to
puncture, no military romanticism for him to wound.
It had finally faded away sometime between 1916 and 1918,
partly because it was exposed by the reality of war itself;
but partly, perhaps, because what he had said about war,
much as it had angered audiences and readers at the time,
had, in the end, had its effect.

# 8 About Doctors

Shaw caught influenza.

"I abstained from medical advice and ammoniated quinine: I treated the fever by enjoying the morning air at an open window in an entirely unprotected condition for a prolonged period before finishing up with a cold bath; I stimulated myself by transitions from the overwhelming heat of the crowded St. James Hall to the chill coolness of Regent Street at night; I wore my lightest attire. I kept out of bed as much as possible."

He recovered, and commented triumphantly, "It is always worth while to fly in the face of that unvenerable survival of witchcraft which calls itself medical science."

*Magic*
"All professions are conspiracies against the laity," said Shaw. The trades-unionism of doctors was not

necessarily worse than that of any other body of men, since doctors were no more dishonest than the average man. But they had extra temptations. One was that they were paid more when their patients were ill than when they were well. The other was that the public was anxious to believe in medical miracles.

The solution to the problem of being paid so much per illness, he said—writing in 1911, thirty-six years before the foundation of the National Health Service—was socialized medicine. "Until the medical profession becomes a body of men trained and paid by the country to keep the country in health it will remain what it is at present; a conspiracy to exploit popular credulity and human suffering." The temptations of a surgeon were stronger than those of a physician. If the patient consulted a surgeon and was told there was nothing much the matter with him, the surgeon only made a few guineas. If he had an operation, the surgeon made fifty. Shaw said, "I cannot knock my shins severely without forcing on some surgeon the difficult question. 'Could I not make better use of a pocketful of guineas than this man is making of his leg?'" And once the leg was off, it was impossible to prove conclusively that the man would not have died if he had kept it. The craze for operations— among patients who enjoyed the drama of being the victim as well as among the surgeons who made a profit— had only been made possible by the invention of chloroform. Before that, no one would have dreamed of having an operation unless it was really necessary. In Shaw's play about the medical profession, *The Doctor's Dilemma,* an old Irish doctor describes what pre-chloroform operations were like.

SIR PATRICK. In my early days you made your man drunk: and the porters and students held him down: and you had to set your teeth and finish the job fast. Nowadays you work at your ease and the pain doesnt come until afterwards, when youve taken your cheque and rolled up your bag and left the house. I tell you, Colly, chloroform has done a lot of mischief. It's enabled every fool to be a surgeon.

Four years before Shaw wrote this play, King Edward VII had developed acute appendicitis on the eve of his coronation. The operation was little known at the time. It got a great deal of publicity, and became regular practice afterwards. In the play, the fashionable surgeon who has invented an original operation of his own makes a fortune out of it.

WALPOLE. You know Mrs. Jack Foljambe, the smart Mrs. Foljambe? I operated at Easter on her sister-in-law, Lady Gorran, and found she had the biggest sac I ever saw: it held about two ounces. Well, Mrs. Foljambe had the right spirit—the genuine hygienic instinct. She couldnt stand her sister-in-law being a clean sound woman, and she simply a whited sepulchre. So she insisted on my operating on her too. And, by George, sir, she hadnt any sac at all. Not a trace! Not a rudiment! I was so taken aback—so interested, that I forgot to take the sponges out and was stitching them up inside her when the nurse missed them.

Doctors have almost unlimited power because of the credulity of the public. The public wants to believe in miracles. They had to have some to believe in because since Darwin had banished God from the universe they could no longer believe in religious ones. Shaw said that they had been better off believing in angels than in germs, and that the consecrated wafer from the Communion table was at least more wholesome than the pill from the chemist's shop. Joan of Arc, who used to carry little children to be baptised of water and the spirit was saner than the modern disciples of compulsory vaccination, who sent the police to force parents to have a disease thrust into their children's veins. Shaw was quite ready to believe that doctors believed in their own magic themselves, before they practised it on other people. Doctors, he said, had recently discovered microbes in the same miraculous way that St. Thomas Aquinas discovered angels. Shaw did not believe they were working on real evidence when they insisted that microbes "caused" diseases. The microbe might equally well be only a symptom of the disease. An unpunctual man is always in a hurry. But that does not prove that hurry is the cause of unpunctuality.

But doctors were able to keep the credulity of the public, not because the cures they prescribed really worked, but because most people were going to recover from their illness, sooner or later, in any case, whether they took the doctor's "cure" or not. In the play, one doctor explains to another how it is done.

RIDGEON. Just rolling in money! I wish you rich G.P.s would teach me how to make some. What is the secret of it?

SCHUTZMACHER. Oh, in my case the secret was simple enough, though I suppose I should have got into trouble if it had attracted any notice. And I'm afraid youll think it rather infra dig.

RIDGEON. Oh, I have an open mind. What was the secret?

SCHUTZMACHER. Well, the secret was just two words.

RIDGEON. Not Consultation Free, was it?

SCHUTZMACHER (*shocked*). No, no. Really!

RIDGEON (*apologetic*). Of course not, I was only joking.

SHUTZMACHER. My two words were simply Cure Guaranteed.

RIDGEON (*admiring*). Cure Guaranteed!

SCHUTZMACHER. Guaranteed. After all, thats what everybody wants from a doctor, isnt it?

RIDGEON. My dear Loony, it was an inspiration. Was it on the brass plate?

SCHUTZMACHER. There was no brass plate. It was a shop window: red, you know, with black lettering. Doctor Leo Schutzmacher, L.R.C.P., M.R.C.S. Advice and medicine sixpence. Cure Guaranteed.

RIDGEON. And the guarantee proved sound nine times out of ten, eh?

SCHUTZMACHER (*rather hurt at so moderate an estimate*). Oh, much oftener than that. You see, most people get well all right if they are careful and you give them a little sensible advice. And the medicine really did them good, Parrish's Chemical Food, phosphates, you know. One tablespoonful to a twelve-ounce bottle of water; nothing better, no matter what the case is.

The reason why most people get better, said Shaw, is because the Life Force maintains a repair department. As soon as a living organism is attacked by an infection of any kind it gets to work influencing the body to work back to normal health again. It heals broken bones and cleans up the foulest infections, in spite of everything that the most foolish doctors and the most unscrupulous curemongers can do to baffle it.

## Moral Judgement

The point of Shaw's play—the actual dilemma of the doctor hero—is whether he should use his power to enforce a moral judgement. In the story a young wife comes to a physician who has recently been knighted for his discovery of a way to cure consumption. She wants him to cure her husband. But the doctor's resources are limited. He can only take ten tuberculous patients into his hospital for the new treatment. He is in the position of a ship's captain, in charge of a life-saving raft already loaded to capacity. If he is to save a new victim one of those already on must be pushed off. The wife pleads that her husband is worth saving above other men, because he is a great artist, whose work will enrich the human race. When the doctor has seen some of the artist's pictures he concedes that this is true, and agrees to take him. But he discovers subsequently that the artist is a rogue, a swindler of a particularly indefensible kind, a bigamist and a blackmailer. His wife—with whom the doctor is beginning to fall in love—believes he is perfect. The doctor has to choose between the undeniably wicked man and a good one, a humble General Practitioner who tries to do his best for his slum patients.

## Medical Scientist

In the play Shaw dealt with the doctor's dilemma, but in the preface, written later, he deals much more seriously with the moral dilemma of the medical scientist. If he could only get knowledge by methods such as vivisection was he justified in doing so? Shaw said that scientists assumed that the right to get knowledge was as absolute as the right to live. But the right to live was, in fact, only conditional in itself, nullified if a man killed someone else. In wartime he might be required to throw away his individual life to save the life of the community. If the scientist really had an absolute right to knowledge, he would be permitted to put his mother in the stove in order to discover how long an adult woman can survive at a temperature of 500° Fahrenheit. It all depends on the point at which society limits the right. In Shaw's view it ought always to stop short of cruelty, whether to an animal or a human being.

He questioned the scientific argument that vivisection was the only way to certain kinds of medical research. He said that Pavlov—a scientist whose work he detested because of his experiments on dogs—could have found out all he needed to know about conditioned reflexes by asking any nursemaid what her charge did when given a jar of jam and a spoon, instead of finding it out by cutting holes in dogs' cheeks. The research scientist of this kind had actually chosen his path to knowledge, and felt that it was consecrated by making a blood sacrifice, like a Druid. There was always another path to knowledge as an alternative to the cruel one, and the man who took the dark one was attracted by it because he had a hidden lust for cruelty.

*Public Health*

Shaw looked upon medical statistics as one of the doctors' methods of getting credulity for their methods. The children of the comfortably-off, who are attended by doctors, have a lower death-rate than those of the poor who (at that time) only had a doctor when they were seriously ill. But the truth was that the children who got the most medical attention were those who were better fed, better housed, and less exposed to infection because their parents were particular about the drainage of their homes. The health of the community did not depend on the healing proficiency of doctors at all, but on its living conditions. The Fabian Society always maintained that disease could not survive in the rationally-managed Utopia which they were planning. In the nineties, they were laughed at as impractical idealists. But they were at least proved right so far as epidemics—which were a major problem of nineteenth-century medicine—were concerned. The kind of outbreak and spread of an epidemic infection which was a commonplace a hundred years ago does not exist today.

## Long Life

When a man keeps his own health and vitality until he dies from an accident at the age of ninety-four as Shaw did, his own apparent eccentricities about his health have to be looked at again and taken seriously. Shaw was a fanatic about his personal habits. He neither drank alcohol, smoked nor ate meat, and criticized those who did. He stopped smoking at an early age, on the grounds that it was useless to pay a sweep to clean the chimneys and then blacken the room oneself. He stopped eating meat when he first discovered Shelley had been a vegetarian. He used to say that meat-eaters were simply cannibals with the heroic dish left out, and that he had no desire to chew the corpses of dead animals. He added that the bull, who is the strongest of animals, is a vegetarian.

By nature he was an ascetic who practised self-discipline because he liked it. His violent dislike of surgery was really an aesthetic one, a revulsion from mutilating the human body. His attack on all forms of vaccination and inoculation was part of his Puritanism. It seemed to him monstrous to infect another human being with a disease, deliberately, whatever the object. If he was alive today, any doctor would advise him to live much the kind of life which he chose for himself long before it was scientifically proved that violent exercise, smoking, alcohol and a high protein diet all shorten life. Many of his most controversial theories about medicine have been proved to be at least partly justified. The theory that he himself thought the most important of all was that man could increase his accepted life-span if only he really wanted to go on living. After his own example, it has to be at least respectfully considered.

# 9 About Bringing up Children

Shaw said, "I cannot too often repeat that although I have no academic qualifications I am in fact much more highly educated than most university scholars."

He did repeat it often enough to suggest he was on the defensive. As a boy he went to a succession of obscure cheap schools and left the last one at fifteen without having distinguished himself in any way. As a man, his friends were intellectuals. Although he protested that he was proud of being self-taught, the past still rankled. He was over ninety before he admitted to the "shame and wounded snobbery" from which he had suffered when sent to school with the sons of petty tradesmen.

*Schools*
As a consequence, he was given to making wild generalizations about education. He said that schools were nothing

but prisons, or at best boy farms where children were sent to be out of their parents' way; that since most of what is taught in schools and colleges is error, therefore it follows that those who have been educated least know most and that the university student who is determined not to study gets most out of the university in the end. This was one of the subjects in which his "G.B.S." personality took over. "G.B.S." was a conscious piece of clowning— a public image which was an exaggerated version of himself. When he was acting this image, he made defiant statements and defended them hotly at all costs. In old age he admitted that "G.B.S.", although the most successful of his fictions, was really a humbug.

"G.B.S." had not a good word to say for any kind of school. He condemned the whole system out of hand. The public-school, he said, produced a nineteenth-century monster, excelling at cricket, tennis and golf, with the ideas of a seventeenth-century squire. All he knew was literary Latin, meaning a kind of Latin which no one ever spoke. If schoolboys must learn a dead language it should at least be Greek, because that was culturally superior. But schools for the poor were worse, because they inculcated a slave mentality. He conceded that there were progressive schools. ("Oh yes: I know all about those wonderful schools that you cannot keep children or even adults out of, and these teachers whom their pupils not only obey without coercion but adore.") But he dismissed them on the grounds that it was impossible to pick up enough enlightened teachers, at a salary of no more than five pounds a week, to convert the millions of scholastic hells into scholastic heavens. When the editor of a progressive educational magazine wrote to him about an experiment in teaching children classical literature at the earliest possible age—an idea which was one of Shaw's hobby-horses—Shaw wrote back, "What you say about education does credit to your feelings: but by the time you have followed the profession of child jailer for a few years you will have no feeling in the matter except perhaps one of savage hatred for the boy in captivity and an intense longing for the day when you shall have saved enough out of your jailer's fees to retire."

*The Noble Savage*
The educational philosophy on which Shaw based this condemnation of all schools was the eighteenth-century one of the "noble savage". This maintained that the "natural man" was good, but was corrupted by the social system; and that therefore the child should be left to develop in his own way. The most famous illustration of the theory is a book by a French political philosopher, Jean-Jacques Rousseau. In it the author describes the upbringing of "Emile" who learns, not from books, but from the world around him. Shaw wanted the Emile-type education adapted to fit modern life. He advocated that children of today should be taught to read, write, reckon and to use their hands, and after that should be set free to educate themselves. "Emile" was a country child and could learn from nature. Shaw suggested that twentieth-century children should learn from their own city civilization, from libraries, art-galleries and museums, and from the theatre. Since he had picked up his own real education in this way, and had become a distinguished critic and man of letters, he thought it should suit everybody. If a child is a born Newton or Shakespeare, he

argued, it will learn the calculus or the art of the theatre without having them forced down its throat.

Shaw's theory fell down—as it does for most philosophers of the "noble savage" school—on the fact that noble savages are impossible to live with. Children in the flesh bored Shaw profoundly. There is not a single study of a child in the whole of his plays. In his ideal world of the future, in *Back to Methuselah*, human beings spend the whole of childhood shut up in an egg. He never had a child of his own, and his view of them was, "They have to be terrorized in the house or let loose to run wild in the streets." He assumed that all parents were longing to get rid of all children for as many hours a day as possible, and that if they were not it simply proved that they were unhealthily possessive. But his idea of children roaming around and educating themselves in the process received a set-back when a group of them attacked him on a walk, calling "Beaver" after him and throwing stones. After that, he decided that they ought to spend their childhood in what he called "child colonies" with their own laws and culture and their own recreations—not on the lines of public school compulsory games, but like the Boy Scouts and Girl Guides. These colonies would not be self-governing, on any sentimental democratic principle, because children were barbarians and the tyranny they would impose on each other would be worse than that of Russia under the Tsars. He pointed out that public schools were able to leave the business of discipline to prefects because they could rely on boys to establish a ruthless and irresistible dictatorship.

### The Child's Rights

Shaw's most solid contribution to theories about child-raising is in the field of human rights rather than practical education. He said that the child's rights as an individual must be respected just as much as those of an adult citizen. The romantic poets, such as Shelley and Wordsworth, who were the only writers to value children in this way since the New Testament, had written of their souls. Shaw put it in his own way. Each child is an experiment of the Life Force, a fresh attempt to produce the just man made perfect, to make humanity divine. Therefore you have no right to treat it either as a little wild beast to be trained or as a pet to be played with. This disposed of the schoolmasters who imprisoned and punished it, the parents who were possessive and spoiled it and the doctrinaire progressives who wanted to try educational experiments upon it as well. "It is the Life Force that has to make the experiment and not the schoolmaster."

He believed that the worst tyranny you can impose upon a child is not physical but mental and moral. If you strike one, you should at least strike it in anger, because a blow in cold blood neither can nor should be forgiven. It is pardonable for an irritable father to swear at his child, or throw his boots at it or send it flying from the room with a cuff or a kick. This merely teaches the child to keep out of his father's way as he would avoid a short-tempered dog or a bull. It is an instructive experience and does no moral damage. But it is quite different for the father to make a moral issue out of the scene, to tell the child solemnly that it is naughty because it annoys him, with the implication that it is offending God by being naughty. This is not only moral tyranny, but blasphemy.

Shaw looked upon ritual whipping of children in the English fashion as obscene. He was delighted when he went to visit Stalin, and Lady Astor—who was in the party—criticized a Soviet nursery school she had seen; and Stalin turned on her furiously and retorted, "In England you *beat* children!" Shaw detested the English interest in the subject of whipping generally. "Can anything be more degrading than the spectacle of a nation reading the biography of Gladstone and gloating over the account of how he was flogged at Eton?" The worst aspect of it all was the perverted pleasure which adults— including parents—took in beating children. Shaw said that the parent who is whitewashing his lust for cruelty under a pretence of reluctance, by saying "This hurts me more than it hurts you," was only adding hypocrisy to his self-indulgence. At least he should be honest about it, and admit, "I beat you because I like beating you and I shall do it whenever I can contrive an excuse for it." But to pretend that this detestable lust represents Divine Wrath maims and blinds the child's soul which is far worse than simply hurting its body.

He shared William Morris's view that, "The question of who are the best people to take charge of children is a very difficult one but it is quite certain that parents are the very worst." Parents are the technicians of human society. But no test of fitness for the job is ever imposed on them, though it is on all other less important professions. Doctors are struck off the register, solicitors off the rolls and parsons unfrocked if they fail to reach the required standard. Shaw wanted to see children taken away from parents who taught them wrong moral values. In a well-run state inefficient amateurs such as parents would not be permitted to handle such an important matter as the character-training of their children. Sex instruction would be given in school. "Children must be taught that the strongest sexual attraction may exist between persons so incompatible in tastes and capacities that they could not endure living together for a week, much less a lifetime, and therefore should not marry one another even though their offspring, which is what Nature aims at, might be eugenically first-rate and their sexual union therefore highly desirable from the public point of view."

Above all, parents should not be allowed to indoctrinate their children with their own private religious faith. Shaw conceded that there might be no harm in their taking the children with them to attend the services of their particular sect, dressed in their best clothes, as a weekly ritual, since it was unlikely that they themselves understood the theology of their own faith well enough to be able to explain it. But real religion is too important to be left to parents, and in any case it is entirely an individual thing. The child's own "inner light" is not likely to be the same one as that of its atheist father or of its sectarian grandfather. Only the State could be trusted to pass on, to the child, the common body of beliefs accepted by the community. Shaw went further than forbidding parents to indoctrinate their own children. He maintained that the State would have to do it, deliberately and ruthlessly, because citizenship, like all forms of corporate life, is impossible without a common religion. He believed that the State could safely be trusted with the child's soul because it must have a strong interest in tolerance and free thought, for its own sake, whereas parents, being possessive about their children, only want them to share their own beliefs. There would of course be opposition to this State proselytizing, Shaw added contemptuously, because in a democracy the people dread good government, as children dread the police. But it is impossible to organize education without dictating religion and politics to children and this the civilized state of the future would have to do, though it would probably never equal the moral tyranny of the Holy Roman Empire.

## Cautionary Tales

When Shaw was a young man and committed whole-heartedly to the "noble savage" ideal of child upbringing, he used to say that children must never be punished and always told the whole truth. As he grew older, he modified his idea. He came to the conclusion that perhaps some way of keeping the noble savages in order might, after all, be necessary. He himself had been coerced into good behaviour by being taught that if he was wicked he would go to hell. There were minor ways of frightening him into virtue, such as that of the cook at his home, who told him that if he was not good—by which she meant if he did not behave with a sole eye to her personal convenience—a cock would come down the chimney. Some kind of fairy-tale, Shaw conceded, might be necessary to persuade children to co-operate. But at least it should be an uplifting, poetic fiction, "lies, but not damned lies". This would cancel out all theories about hell, and much of the Old Testament. The Old Testament stories, if taught as articles of faith, implied that polygamy, the slaughter of prisoners of war, blood sacrifices and human sacrifices were divinely appointed institutions. But children should study the Old Testament as a work of literature, a collection of chronicles, poems, oracles and political fulminations on the same footing as the travels of Marco Polo.

Sooner or later, the child was bound to discover that the fairy-tales employed to teach it good behaviour were falsehoods. Shaw looked back and saw that when this had happened to him, the damage it had done was in shaking his faith in the infallibility of his parents. He decided that it would be much better if the adults around the child told him the truth about the cautionary tales on which it had been brought up before the child discovered it. He suggested that this should be done systematically, by a series of "coming of age" disillusionments. At each stage, the child should be informed that it was now old enough to know that the previous legend had been just that. Children would proceed from stage to stage of disillusionment as they now move up from form to form in school.

### Freedom from Home

"Home is the girl's prison and the woman's workhouse," said Shaw, in *Maxims for Revolutionists*. Once children were old enough to want to get away from home, he was interested in them. In *Misalliance*, the daughter of the house sums up what Shaw supposed all adolescents must feel about their home. "Oh home! home! family! duty! how I loathe them! How I'd like to see them all blown to bits!" In *Fanny's First Play* the well-brought-up young people of conventional families escape from home and get into trouble with the police and are put in prison and come back much better for the experience. Shaw comments, in the preface to the play, "The young had better have their souls awakened by disgrace, capture by the police and a month's hard labour than drift along from their cradles to their graves doing what other people do for no other reason than that other people do it, and knowing nothing of good and evil, of courage and cowardice, or indeed anything but how to keep hunger and concupiscence and fashionable dressing within the bounds of good taste." Parents and children should part from each other as soon as the child has reached the age at which it no longer requires physical protection, not only because the child needs freedom, but because the relationship is an embarrassing one. As the father in *Misalliance* says, "You cant get over the fearful shyness of it." This father could not manage to tell his son about the dangers and temptations of sex. "I just had to leave books in his way: and I felt awful when I did it." The relation between the young and the old ought to be an innocent one, but it never can be between parents and children. "Depend on it, in a thousand years it'll be considered bad form to know who your father and mother are." Twenty-three years later, when Aldous Huxley wrote his novel of a future Utopia, any mention of one's parents is an obscenity. When the heroine's boy friend is embarrassed, during his love-making, she reflects, "He couldn't look more upset if I'd made a dirty joke—asked him who his mother was, or something like that."

Most philosophers who write about child upbringing are dogged by subjectivity. They look back on their own childhood and assume that their problems are the universal ones, shared by all children. Shaw was no exception. His own mother had been openly bored with the business of bringing up a family, so he assumed that all parents were. He had hated his school, so all children hated all schools. He was self-taught, so all children should be. Education was one of the few subjects over which he did not trouble to study the facts carefully before writing about it. During his lifetime there was an educational revolution which transformed schools and a social one which changed the ordinary home out of all recognition, but he hardly noticed either. To the end of his life he continued to write about child upbringing as it had been when he was young.

But his passionate belief that the community owes the child its freedom from physical assault and from mental indoctrination has stood up to the test of time. British law has always been notoriously backward about the child's rights. It has persisted in putting the parent's right to authority first. The National Society for the Prevention of Cruelty to Children was necessary simply because children had no legal protection against their own parents. It was founded after social reformers had found that the only way to penalize cruel parents was to take the child to court as an "animal" which had been ill-treated. Dogs were protected, but not children. Shaw said that parents and children were two different classes of society, confronting each other, with all the political power on one side and slavery on the other. Society relied upon the bond of natural affection to keep the political power within bounds, but it did not always work out that way. He wanted the child to have a separate legal status of its own.

Although his whole theory of the noble savage and the right of a child to be independent of schoolmasters and parents was a defence of human liberties, he was determined that the state must have far more authority over the child than it ever has had up till now. He favoured complete indoctrination of all children with the authorized beliefs laid down by the government. It is part of his detachment from real-life children that it never seems to have occurred to him that moral and mental compulsion and pressure, whether they are applied by the home or the school or the state, feel much the same at the receiving end.

# 10 About the English

Shaw said, "Personally I like Englishmen much better than Irishmen (no doubt because they make more of me) just as many Englishmen like Frenchmen better than Englishmen. But I never think of an Englishman as my countryman."

He showed his appreciation of his own native land, he said, in the usual Irish way by getting out of it as soon as possible. He came to London at the age of twenty and did not set foot in Ireland again for nearly thirty years and then only to please his wife. ("How many of all the millions that have left Ireland have ever come back or wanted to come back?") To him Ireland stood for all the fecklessness and inefficiency of his childhood home, for failure and obscurity and boredom and a particular kind of mental laziness. In *John Bull's Other Island* the exiled Irishman who has made good in England shrinks from going back there. He dreads the dreaming—"the torturing, heartscalding never-satisfying dreaming". No debauchery, he says, that ever coarsened and brutalized an Englishman can take the worth out of a man as dreaming does out of the Irishman. "It saves thinking. It saves working." Above all he dreads the laughter, the eternal flippancy and derision so that "when you come at last to a country where men take a question seriously and give a serious answer to it, you deride them for having no sense of humor, and plume yourself on your own worthlessness as if it made you better than them."

To Shaw London was an escape from the dreaming futility of Dublin. Even in his first years of poverty and unemployment in England, the social climate suited him better—the toughness, the struggle to keep his head above water, the being surrounded by people who meant to get on in the world. He was impatient with the romantic English idea of the Irish as a race of picturesque and lovable Celts. "When people talk about the Celtic race, I feel as if I could burn down London. That sort of rot does more harm than ten Coercion Acts." He said that the reason why Irishmen played up to the Englishman's image of them was that it enabled them to loaf and drink and sponge and brag by flattering the Englishman's sense of moral superiority.

Shaw always had a kind of love-hate relationship with the country of his adoption. He abused the English for their hypocrisy and pompousness and sanctimonious moral attitudes, but he took them seriously and settled down among them without a backward look, as a man who has risen above his source leaves his family behind, only compelled to remember and help them, from a kind of exasperated loyalty, if they are in serious trouble. Any mention of Home Rule aroused a reflex patriotism, and when his fellow-countryman, Roger Casement, was tried for treason during the 1914 war, Shaw wrote a speech for him to deliver at his trial, reiterating Ireland's history of oppression at the hands of the English. "But would you believe it? Casement flatly refused and lost the greatest chance in history. They hanged him, as I told him they would in spite of his costly lawyers."

The only thing about Ireland which he really loved was its countryside. He said in old age that the happiest day of his life had been the one on which his mother told him that they were going to move from Dublin into the country. There is virtually no poetical description in the whole of Shaw's works. When he tries to write a speech for the poet in *Candida* to make to the woman he loves, he fails lamentably. The only time he succeeds is in writing about the Irish landscape—"that soft moist air . . . those white springy roads, those misty rushes and brown bogs . . . those hillsides of granite rocks and magenta heather. You've no such colors in the sky, no such lure in the distances, no such sadness in the evenings."

## Flattering the English

But in fact his habit of satirising the English character in his plays started by being the very kind of concealed flattery for which he abused the Irish loafers who sponged on the English by making them feel superior. He wrote *John Bull's Other Island* to illustrate the relationship between the English and Irish. The Irish mock the naïve and pompous Englishman who goes over to show them how to run their village. The laugh is always against the

Englishman. But it is the insensitive, ridiculous Englishman who gets things done. Shaw said he meant it as a moral lesson for the Irish. But the English accepted it tolerantly, perfectly willing to see themselves as absurd provided they were also represented as "cheerful, robust, good-natured, free from envy and above all as successful muddlers-through in business and in love." However much Shaw mocked the English on the stage, English audiences loved it. Shaw said that they smacked their lips over his criticisms because these gave them a chance to prove that they could take a caricature of themselves with large-minded good humour. What really flatters a man is that you think it worth taking the trouble to flatter him at all, and making jokes about him to his face implies that there is no real sting in them, or else that his position is so impregnable that he can afford to permit it. Most of what Shaw said about the English character is no more than the work of a jester whose job it is to make sly fun of his employer. It was a stage trick, as old as Shakespeare. In *Hamlet* the gravedigger says that the prince has been sent to England because he is mad and " 'twill not be noticed there; there the men are as mad as he." Shakespeare knew it was always worth a laugh. So did Shaw.

He first used it in *The Man of Destiny* in which the heroine suddenly announces that she had an English grandfather, simply in order to give the dramatist the opportunity to put a long description of the English character into the mouth of Napoleon. This begins with a remark said to have been made by the real-life Napoleon that the English are a nation of shopkeepers. The Englishman, says Shaw's Napoleon, never admits he is in the wrong because he does everything on principle. He is never at a loss for an effective moral attitude. He supports his king on loyal principles but cuts his king's head off on republican principles. When he wants to do anything he does not do it at once but waits until there comes into his mind a mysterious burning conviction that it is his moral duty to do it. "When he wants a new market for his adulterated Manchester goods, he sends a missionary to teach the natives the Gospel of Peace. The natives kill the missionary; he flies to arms in defence of Christianity; fights for it, conquers for it and takes the market as a reward from heaven."

It was this assumption of moral superiority which was Shaw's chief target. It was a common accusation against Britain in her imperialist days—the "perfidious Albion" who was always sanctimoniously in the right. Audiences appreciated the speech in *The Man of Destiny* and Shaw repeated the trick in *Caesar and Cleopatra*, but less seriously and more good-naturedly. In this play, Caesar has a British slave, Britannus, who is a caricature of a modern Englishman, set in the time of the Roman conquest. He explains to Cleopatra why the Britons stain themselves with woad.

CLEOPATRA. Is it true that when Caesar caught you on that island you were painted all over blue?
BRITANNUS. Blue is the color worn by all Britons of good standing. In war we stain our bodies blue; so that though our enemies may strip us of our clothes and our lives, they cannot strip us of our respectability.

Britannus is shocked when Theodotus, a court official, explains that in the royal family of Egypt the brother and sister nearest the throne always marry each other.

THEODOTUS. Ptolemy and Cleopatra are born king and consort just as they are born brother and sister.

BRITANNUS (*shocked*). Caesar: this is not proper.

THEODOTUS (*outraged*). How!

CAESAR (*recovering his self-possession*). Pardon him, Theodotus; he is a barbarian and thinks that the customs of his island and his tribe are the laws of nature.

BRITANNUS. On the contrary, Caesar, it is these Egyptians who are barbarians and you do wrong to encourage them. I say it is a scandal.

When critics complained that a Briton of twenty centuries ago would hardly have the same characteristics as a modern one, Shaw retorted that it was climate that made national character and that Great Britain, Ireland and America, who were all the same stock, were three of the most distinctly marked nationalities under the sun because they all lived in different climates.

Other Victorian writers had satirized the respectability of the Englishman, and his pomposity and love of moralizing. But in *Back to Methuselah* Shaw started on a new theme of his own, that the English never really grow up. In the play, England of the future is theoretically governed by its own statesman but really the government is run by a Chinese sage who does all the work so that the English can devote themselves to outdoor sports and flirtations with women. The sage's attitude to the British president is one of calm contempt.

CONFUCIUS. People like you. They like cheerful good-natured barbarians. They have elected you President five times in succession. They will elect you five times more. *I* like you. You are better company than a dog or a horse because you can speak.

BURGE-LUBIN. Am I a barbarian because you like me?
CONFUCIUS. Surely. Nobody likes me; I am held in awe.
Capable persons are never liked. I am not likeable; but
I am indispensable.

When it is discovered that the Archbishop of Canterbury and the Domestic Minister are secret Longlivers,
each approaching three centuries old, Confucius realises
that he has always known they were the only truly adult
persons among his English acquaintances. The usual
English face is not an adult one, any more than the
English mind is. The President protests. He reminds
Confucius of the Kipling picture of the English as a race
divinely appointed to rule over backward nations and to
teach them English institutions. Confucius says that the
highest compliment you can pay any people is to say that
they are not grown up. The highest creatures take the
longest to mature and are the most helpless in their infancy.

CONFUCIUS. Your maturity is so late that you never attain
to it. You have to be governed by races which are
mature at forty. That means that you are potentially
the most highly-developed race on earth, and would
actually be the greatest if you could live long enough to
attain maturity.

Like Burge-Lubin in the play, English audiences were
delighted with this picture of themselves once they
grasped it. "That explains everything. We are just a lot of
schoolboys; theres no denying it." It explains the
national passion for sport, the lack of appreciation of
serious art and the likeable boyishness. (Santayana's description of the British Empire—"Never has the world

been ruled by such a sweet, just, boyish master"—was still ringing in English ears.) Burge-Lubin's conclusion was, "It's true: it's absolutely true. But some day we'll grow up: and then, by Jingo, we'll shew 'em."

But in *Saint Joan* the joke about the English ceases to be a joke. The stage trick gives place to a sincere and deeply-felt indictment. De Stogumber, the English chaplain, has all the faults which Shaw had ridiculed in other plays. He is romantic about war, and believes that the English are never fairly defeated. Like Britannus, he looks upon English beliefs as the laws of the universe. "How can what an Englishman believes be heresy? It is a contradiction in terms." He is pitifully snobbish, boasting that there are only six cousins between him and a barony. He is so unintellectual that he cannot follow the arguments of the French Bishop. Above all, he is passionately and sentimentally patriotic. The Earl of Warwick has to apologize for him when he calls the bishop a traitor. "It does not mean in England what it does in France. In your language traitor means betrayer: one who is perfidious, treacherous, unfaithful, disloyal. In our country it means simply one who is not wholly devoted to our English interests." At first the chaplain's absurdities are pure comedy, just as the same qualities in the English character had been to Shaw, before the 1914 war. But in 1914, the Imperialistic fervour of the British, which had been waning since the South African war, flickered up again into its last serious blaze. It was as though they wanted to reassure themselves that all the ideals of the late-Victorian era—the colonialism and the flag-worshipping and the admiration of military virtues—were worth fighting for. The hysterical war-fever of 1914 almost startled the

English people themselves. It horrified Shaw. It was this making of the war into a crusade—a Holy War—that he attacked in "Common-Sense About the War". He himself was completely untouched by the 1914 mood and it was incomprehensible to him that fellow-intellectuals and friends were part of it, instead of sharing his detachment. He was accustomed to be criticized for sniping at the British way of life, and throve on it, as most controversial writers do. But when his public turned on him with real abuse and resentment he was bewildered. They had enjoyed being told they were arrogant and hypocritically moral, in his pre-war plays. But when he wrote that "of two insufferably conceited and aggressive peoples, the English and the Germans, the Germans are to be preferred, not as being morally better, but as being more frank and consequently less irritating about their wickedness" there was such an outbreak of hate against him that he obligingly offered to write the kind of articles editors really wanted to print against him, himself; for instance, "That callous clown, Bernard Shaw, who takes a malign delight in distracting our attention from the unbearable horrors which threaten us and laughs at the handless and eyeless victims of the Hun in the very faces of English mothers who are sending their sons to the front——" In *Heartbreak House* he had called pre-war England, "this silly house, this strangely happy house, this agonizing house, this house without foundations". But it came to an end in 1914 and was never the same again. The war was a traumatic experience for Shaw, and he never wrote so light-heartedly about British idiosyncrasies after it. The English chaplain in *Saint Joan* is a caricature of an Englishman, in the same way that Britannus was. But all the characteristics which begin by being comic become serious and evil. His blind patriotism and crusading fervour end up as hideous cruelty. In contrast to the Inquisitor and the Bishop, de Stogumber wants to see Joan burned alive. He says he is so devoted to England that if she is not destroyed by the authorities he will fling his cassock to the devil and take arms himself and strangle the accursed witch with his own hands. At the end of her trial, when she is condemned to be burned, he is hysterical with joy.

THE CHAPLAIN. Into the fire with the witch (*he rushes at her and helps the soldiers to push her out*).

He comes back from watching the burning a broken man.

THE CHAPLAIN. You madden yourself with words: you damn yourself because it feels grand to throw oil on the flaming hell of your own temper. But when it is brought home to you: when you see the thing you have done: when it is blinding your eyes, stifling your nostrils, tearing your heart, then—then—(*falling on his knees*) O God, take away this sight from me!

In the Epilogue, when Joan comes back in a dream, twenty-five years later, de Stogumber is a crazy old parish priest, hardly remembering what it was that drove him insane. He still cannot face up to reality, after a lifetime of repenting since. His last word to Joan is, "Oh do not come back; you must not come back. I must die in peace. Give us peace in our time, O Lord."

# 11   About the Theatre

At the time when Shaw was a dramatic critic, the theatre
had taken a new lease of life.  It was a time of prosperity,
of the rise of the new middle class and of a new public
with enough free time and money to go to plays.  Matinées
were still a novelty.  They were put on for people who
wanted to come up from the suburbs and see some kind of
a show.  Improved transport made it possible for
audiences to cross London or come in from Wimbledon
and Golders' Green, quickly and easily.  Theatre-going
had become respectable.  A nonconformist parson put on
an amateur Christmas pantomime in his mission hall
without raising the storm of protest that would certainly
have followed a few years earlier.  Clergy began to preach
about the possible good influence of the stage, and praised
noble-minded actor-managers who tried to elevate its tone.
People talked about it as they do about television today.

*Theatre of the Nineties.*

All this meant that the kind of plays which had pleased earlier, less respectable audiences would no longer do. Managers scrapped the old sensational melodramas, such as *Murder in the Red Barn*, and settled down to a fixed pattern suitable for their public. First there was Shakespeare, which not only entertained them, but made them feel virtuous, slightly smug, because they were patronizing the top English classic. Shakespeare was almost a religion. His works were above criticism, and murder and adultery were not the same when they occurred in a Shakespeare play as in any other. The famous actor-managers, who dominated the theatre, used to tailor the plays in order to give themselves good parts. Secondly, there were historical plays, often in verse, but always in a particular "period" English which was the way theatre-goers supposed that everyone had spoken who had been born half a century or more before themselves. Thirdly there were farces, and these could be slightly "naughty", provided they limited the naughtiness to suggestiveness, in order that it could pass over the heads of the pure.

But the basic of the late-Victorian stage was what was called the "well-made play". When Shaw was a dramatic critic he assured his readers that any of them could write a "well-made play" themselves, provided they followed his simple instructions. They must begin by choosing "the situation", and the easiest of all was that it should be the situation of an innocent person accused of a crime. If the person was a woman, she must be (wrongly) convicted of adultery. If it was a young officer he must be accused of selling secrets to the enemy, through the machinations of a beautiful spy. If it was a wife, she must be banished from home and disguise herself as a nursemaid to come back and nurse her sick child, unrecognized by the rest of the family. You introduce your characters in the first act, by elaborate explanations on the part of servants. In the second act, you have the "situation"; and in the third "the denouement" which consists of clearing up the misunderstandings and getting the audience out of the theatre as best you can.

The bourgeois audiences who came up from the suburbs liked to see how the aristocracy lived, and the aristocracy liked to see their lives mirrored on the stage, so the well-made play took place in titled homes, just as the "drawing-room plays" used to be set in Surrey mansions and gracious-living week-end cottages, before the kitchen-sink school moved in to the theatre of the mid-twentieth-century.

Into this world of watered-down Shakespeare, costume dramas and tales of the upper classes resisting adultery, Ibsen burst like a revolutionary.

### Ibsen

He wrote about ordinary people living in suburbs or provincial towns, and about the kind of problem that really wrecked their everyday lives. His settings were, like himself, Norwegian, but as Shaw said, if you wanted to find an Ibsen-type household you need only jump out of a train anywhere between Wimbledon and Haslemere, walk into the first villa you came to, and there you were.

The first Ibsen play to be produced in England was *A Doll's House.* It is about an idyllic marriage, in which the husband is still passionately in love with his wife after eight years of marriage and three children. He idolizes her, and she plays up to his image of her. But their relationship completely collapses when he discovers that she is in the hands of a blackmailer. She owes a large sum of money which she is paying off in instalments. Her creditor is an employee of her husband and threatens to expose the fact that she forged a guarantee to get the money unless she coaxes her husband to keep him on and promote him.

In Ibsen's play, unlike the conventional ones, the wife is guilty, although she lied and cheated only to get money which they needed urgently when her husband was ill. The climax of it is when she realizes the falseness of their partnership. Although the blackmailer withdraws and they could go on as before, she decides to break up her home and leave her husband to find some kind of reality in life. The husband cannot understand it.

HELMER. How unreasonable and how ungrateful you are, Nora! Have you not been happy here?

NORA. No, I have never been happy. I thought I was, but it has never really been so.

HELMER. Not—not happy!

NORA. No, only merry. And you have always been so kind to me. But our home has been nothing but a playroom. I have been your doll-wife just as at home I was papa's doll-child; and here the children have been my dolls. I thought it great fun when you played with me, just as they thought it great fun when I played with them. That is what our marriage has been.

Not only the British public was shocked by this play, but theatre audiences of Norway, France and Denmark. The plot sounds mild enough today. In the nineties it was almost blasphemous. It threatened the illusions by which people lived, the pictures of an ideal marriage, the sacred duty of a woman to put her husband and children before her own rights as an individual. In their hearts audiences know that the things that threaten a marriage are not glamorous adultery and beautiful spies, but problems like trying to find the money to pay off a debt out of the housekeeping allowance. But they did not want to be faced with the truth when they went to the theatre.

The other play which had appalled European audiences but was banned in England was Ibsen's *Ghosts*, the story of a devotedly moral wife who goes back to her husband on the advice of her local parson, and gets venereal disease and bears a child who inherits it and goes mad, as a reward for her morality. The critics called Ibsen's plays, "as foul and filthy concoctions as have ever been allowed to disgrace the boards of an English theatre", and "just a wicked nightmare". "Get out from the moral leper house and tell us something of the cleanliness that is next to Godliness, something of the trials and struggles of the just, the sorely-tried, the tempted and the pure," one begged the theatre-managers, in a rhetorical article about the state of the theatre. Another said crushingly, "Outside a silly clique there is not the slightest interest in the Scandinavian humbug or all his works."

Shaw was not only part of this clique but one of the leaders of it. Ever since he was first introduced to the works of Ibsen, he had realized that this was the way the theatre should be used; to make people think, to make them uneasy because they began to see the difference between the way life is and what it ought to be. It was a place for stimulating discussion, for understanding other points of view. Shaw added a quality of his own—it should be a place for teaching by laughter and excitement as well.

Ibsen was a grave sombre Scandinavian who found life and society tragic. Shaw was a witty, light-hearted Irishman who believed that human beings were not merely in control of their own destiny, but could re-arrange it and the world around them if they would only pull themselves together and look facts in the face. Ibsen liked to underline his moralizing by tragedy. Shaw loved to round his off by a sudden comic anti-climax. When Ibsen tells the story of Hedda Gabler who is afraid of life and cannot escape from her own limitations, although she longs to, he ends with her suicide, and the nearest we get to lightening the tragedy is the heavy irony of the respectable man who gets the last line of the play.

TESMAN (*shrieking to Brack*). Shot herself! Shot herself in the temple! Think of it!
BRACK (*half-collapsed in the easy-chair*). But, merciful God! One doesn't *do* that kind of thing!

But when Shaw presents a tortured dreamer, in the expatriate Irishman of *John Bull's Other Island*, he brings him promptly down to earth. Larry Doyle has summed up the bitterness of the Irishman's inability to convert dreaming into action in a long and moving speech. "When youre young, you exchange drinks with other young men; and you exchange vile stories with them; and as youre too futile to be able to help or cheer them, you chaff and sneer and taunt them for not doing the things you darent do yourself. And all the time you laugh,

laugh, laugh! eternal derision, eternal envy, eternal folly, eternal fouling and staining and degrading . . ."

BROADBENT (*roused to intense earnestness by Doyle's eloquence*). Never despair, Larry. There are great possibilities for Ireland. Home Rule will work wonders under English guidance.

DOYLE (*pulled up short, his face twitching with a reluctant smile*). Tom; why do you select my most tragic moments for your most irresistible strokes of humor?

Ibsen's genius, as Shaw saw it, was that he questioned accepted morality. The average "well-made play", Shaw said, was a fable without a moral. It simply went on repeating the same platitudes. A typical plot tells how a villain tries to separate an honest pair of betrothed lovers, to gain the hand of the woman by calumny and to ruin the man by forgery. Everyone knows that forgery and seduction are not socially-acceptable activities. There is nothing for the audience to discuss. Talking and thinking about a play of this kind is moral babble. What a play ought to do is to raise problems of conduct and character, of personal importance to the audience, to hold up accepted morality and revalue it. Ibsen did exactly this in all of his earlier plays. Was the mother in *Ghosts* right to go back to her lawfully-wedded husband and thus condemn her son to go through life ridden by a terrible and killing disease? Was the heroine of *A Doll's House* wrong to break free from a false and hypocritical married relationship? In Shaw's picture of the enlightened future, in *Back to Methuselah*, Ibsen has been canonised and is now known as Saint Henrik Ibsen. Around the base of the monument erected to his memory is the inscription, "I came not to call sinners, but the righteous, to repentance."

Shaw was under the spell of Ibsenism during all the first part of his playwriting career. In *Widowers' Houses*, his first play, he wrote of slum-landlordism. In *Mrs Warren's Profession* he dissected the economic system which produced prostitution. In *Arms and the Man* he exposed the falseness of the romantic conception of war. In *Candida* he was overhung by the "Doll's House" theme, but as he was (unlike Ibsen) incapable of creating a silly heroine, his "Candida", who is as strong-minded and well-balanced as any of those he created, succeeds in getting her own over-idealized marriage relationship onto a more realistic basis and so achieves a happy ending. The strength of Shaw's treatment of his subjects came from his discovery of Ibsen. But his tremendous influence on the English theatre was because of his own gifts for laughter and drama. Audiences went home after an evening of Ibsen sadder and wiser than when they started out. They went home from a Shaw play lighter of heart, and wiser as well. One critic summed up Shaw as "the laughing Ibsen".

## Shakespeare

Shaw's long anti-Shakespeare campaign started as a journalistic "gimmick", as we should call it today. He and the editor of the *Saturday Review* launched a campaign against the semi-religious worship of Shakespeare among actor-managers and audiences. They called this worship "Bardolatry". To audiences of the nineties Shakespeare was sacrosanct. It was blasphemy to suggest that any word he wrote could possibly be less than perfect. The

Lyceum theatre was one of the temples of Shakespeare-worship. Shaw wrote that it was "exclusively occupied with the works of a seventeenth-century author in whose social views no educated and capable person today has the faintest interest". Shakespeare, he added, had no creed and no programme, and his plots were all reach-me-downs. This attack on the Shakespeare-mystique made critics and audiences so indignant that, even if Shaw had wanted to back down, he could not have brought himself to do it. Angry opposition always made him more stubborn. He never forgot the slogan of his political-speaking period, "Never argue, repeat your assertion." He admitted, when he was old, that the Shakespeare-baiting campaign had got slightly out of hand, in response to the storm of abuse it caused. In fact he never claimed that he himself, as a writer, was "better than Shakespeare" but had, he said, added a question-mark to the phrase. He had been saturated in Shakespeare's works since he was a boy, and went to Stratford-on-Avon so often that he came to think of it as a supplementary birth-place of his own. Shakespeare had reached the summit of dramatic art, just as Michelangelo had of fresco, so it was impossible for anyone to be better than Shakespeare. What he did claim was to be Shakespeare's successor.

But he had one real fault to find with Shakespeare—his pessimism. Shakespeare, said Shaw, did not believe, as Bunyan believed, that there was a celestial city at the end of the pilgrim's path. He did not think, as Ibsen did, that man could live more nobly by transforming his surroundings, nor, as Shaw himself did, that human beings could change the destiny of the human race, through evolution, by making up their minds to progress. Shakespeare saw his characters as helpless creatures trapped in the terror of a drunken nightmare—"We are such stuff as dreams are made on and our little life is rounded with a sleep."

### Naturalism in the Theatre

It was the "Bardolatry" of the nineteenth-century theatre which bogged down all historical plays into a stage tradition of speech in "period" English. No historical character on the Victorian stage ever talked or reasoned or acted in an everyday way, but only in a special stagey one which was traditional. When audiences went to see a historical play, they did not expect to feel personally involved, or to identify themselves with the characters or their problems. They simply listened and watched, untouched, feeling it was more an improving history lesson than an emotional experience. One of the stand-bys of Victorian actor-managers, for instance, was Bulwer-Lytton's *Richelieu or The Conspiracy*. In it, the villain is trying to take a helpless girl out of Richelieu's protection. The stagey dialogue is typical.

RICHELIEU. She shall not stir!
BARADAS. You are not of her kindred—— An orphan——
RICHELIEU. And her country is her mother!
BARADAS. The country is the King!

Shaw parodied this kind of language in *The Admirable Bashville or Constancy Unrewarded*.

LYDIA. Welcome, dear cousin, to my London house. Of late you have been chary of your visits.
LUCIAN. I have been greatly occupied of late.

The minister to whom I act as scribe
In Downing Street was born in Birmingham,
And, like a thoroughbred commercial statesman,
Splits his infinitives, which I, poor slave,
Must re-unite.

But when he wrote his first historical play, he broke away from the tradition and presented Napoleon as thinking and talking in the same way as the audience did.

NAPOLEON (*passionately*). You idiot; I'll have you shot for losing those despatches; I'll have you blown from the mouth of a cannon; nothing less could make any impression on you. (*Baying at him*). Do you hear? Do you understand?

Shaw's Caesar, the noblest and loftiest of all his characters, is, all the same, human enough for any man in the audience to identify with him.

RUFIO (*contemptuously*). Your birthday! You always have a birthday when there is a pretty girl to be flattered or an ambassador to be conciliated. We had seven of them in ten months last year.
CAESAR (*contritely*). It is true, Rufio! I shall never break myself of these petty deceits.

In *Saint Joan*, Shaw conveys that Joan is a country girl come to court by making her talk in the idiom of a Lancashire mill-girl.

JOAN. Where be Dauphin?
BLUEBEARD (*condescendingly*). You are in the presence of the Dauphin.

*Joan looks at him sceptically for a moment, scanning him up and down to make sure. Dead silence, all watching her. Fun dawns in her face*

JOAN. Coom, Bluebeard! Thou canst not fool me. Where be Dauphin?

Today, no playwright would think of trying to write a historical play in "period" English. During the last forty years there has been a spate of naturalistic plays about historical characters, but they all think and act and talk in twentieth-century idiom. This trend was invented and first put onto the English stage by Shaw. It is one of his often-forgotten contributions to the theatre.

*National Theatre*
Shaw thought that the theatre ought to be "a factory of thought, a prompter of conscience and elucidator of social conscience, an armory against despair and dulness, a temple of the Ascent of Man". The mediaeval church used to be the nation's soul. It had, in fact, used the drama itself to put across its message. This was what Shaw wanted the theatre to be. He used it as his own pulpit. He believed that a National Theatre was as necessary as a national church. In 1910 a fund was being raised for this project. As his subscription to the cause, Shaw wrote a play, *The Dark Lady of the Sonnets*, in which he pictures an imaginary meeting between Queen Elizabeth I and Shakespeare. Most of it consists of a joke at Shakespeare's expense, by which many of Shakespeare's most-quoted lines are used in the ordinary course of conversation by the queen and jotted down by the poet so that he may

pass them off as his own in his plays. But the last lines (in which Shakespeare begs the queen to endow a national theatre, in which his plays can be done—because theatre-managers will only do commercially-successful ones, such as "a murder or a plot or some naughty tale of wantonness") illustrate Shaw's real feeling about the mission of the drama. Queen Elizabeth says she dare not endow a theatre herself because the unruly Puritans would make trouble if she did. But she adds that when England becomes really civilized, it will have a national one.

ELIZABETH. I tell thee, Master Will, it will be three hundred years and more before my subjects learn that man cannot live by bread alone but by every word that cometh from the mouth of those whom God inspires.

# 12 About the Future

"I set myself down as a Creative Evolutionist," said
Shaw, when asked to define his faith. He had only been
three years old when Darwin's *Origin of Species* rocked
the foundations of Victorian beliefs, but the effects—the
clamour, the denunciations, the efforts to find some kind
of a new foundation—lasted on for half a century afterwards. Evolution was not a discovery of Darwin's. It
had been in the air, a subject for speculation, for a long
time, just in the way that ideas about atomic power were
before 1945. But Darwin's summary and evidence had a
sudden impact. His conclusion that man and monkey had
evolved from a common ancestor not only invalidated
the book of Genesis, but, as Samuel Butler put it, had
"banished God from the universe". What Shaw called
the "dismal creed" of Darwin's successors was that if a
giraffe's neck was not long enough to reach its food, it

died, leaving the adequately-necked giraffes to carry on
the race—that is, said Shaw, that improvement of any
species can come only through senseless accidents which
must eventually be wiped out by other senseless accidents.
He came to believe himself that the species—including
man—were the work of a creative force. He went back
to the theories of a Frenchman, Lamarck, who had said
that the species changed by willing themselves to, in the
same way that a baby crawling about the floor becomes a
boy walking upright, that is by taking the decision and
persisting in it. Shaw combined Darwin and Lamarck
to build up a theory—a religion, he called it—of his own.

In the years when Darwin had set everyone discussing
the destiny of the human race, authors wrote what we
should now call science fiction about it, in the same
way that mid-twentieth-century authors wrote "space-
shockers" once it began to seem possible that man should
explore space. If the pre-monkey had become a man, as
Darwin said, then what would the man become, in time?
Shaw was interested in what man—inspired by this
creative force which meant him to evolve and improve—
would make of himself. In 1903 he set out to put the idea
into a play, *Man and Superman*. He meant it to be a
dramatic parable of Creative Evolution showing how man
is born to do the work of the Life Force, by using the
legend of Don Juan, famous for his seductions of women,
and turning it into a morality play about man's real
biological duty. But Shaw said, "being then at the height
of my invention and comedic talent, I decorated it too
brilliantly and lavishly". He surrounded the main theme
with a comedy, and the theme itself is only put in such a
long act that it has to be played separately. In 1920 he

decided (rather prematurely as it turned out) that he must put his belief into dramatic form before he died. So he wrote *Back to Methuselah* which he hoped would do the same for the religion of Creative Evolution as the religious paintings of the fifteenth century did for the Christian church.

Lamarck had thought that changes and improvements could only be seen in the species over a period of time (that is never in individuals) because of the shortness of individual life. This is really the theme of Shaw's play. If man could live longer, he could evolve in his own lifetime. And unless he could do this, according to Shaw, there was no hope of his really becoming the superman who would be the next step upward, assuming you had started at the monkey and gone on to the man. Whether this idea was scientifically sound or not (and Darwin's theories have been so much challenged, since then, that it is out of date) at any rate it was dramatically a perfect idea. Therefore *Back to Methuselah* lives on, in its own right, as a work of art, still delighting audiences who would have to think before they remembered what Darwin said and who never heard of Lamarck at all.

This longevity of the future, which to Shaw represented the best hope of the human race, would, he thought, start suddenly, not gradually. He said that when you learn to ride a bicycle success does not come bit by bit. For days you will yourself to balance and ride but fall off and fail. Then suddenly one day you can ride and after that you can always ride. He thought the capacity to live long would come in the same way. Human beings would get the will to survive for three hundred years or so, and suddenly one or two of them would find they could do it.

In the play, the two discoverers of this new scientific theory tell it to a party politician who had hoped they were going to confide some discovery which he could include in his election programme.

BURGE. Do you mean to say that you have nothing more practical to offer than the mere wish to live longer? Why, if people could live by merely wishing to, we should all be living for ever already!

No one will take the discoverers seriously. Even the intellectual young daughter of one of them, who has supported them up till then, deserts them when they say that the first Longliver might be anyone—even their own parlourmaid.

In the next act it is two and a half centuries later and the parlourmaid has survived. She has to keep it a secret, because everyone would consider her a monster if they knew, and she thinks she is the only longliver in the world, until she discovers that the Archbishop of Canterbury is the same man who was a humble curate in her own parish at the time when the theory was first discovered. (From a dramatic point of view this is the best act of the play-cycle, because it has the never-failing dramatic formula of the audience knowing a wonderful secret before the players on the stage realize it.)

In the next part of the play it is 3,000 A.D. and the Longlivers are a separate race, visited by tourists and people who want wise advice from them. When H. G. Wells wrote stories about the future of man, he was most interested in the scientific and engineering discoveries they would have made. (He wrote a description of a future war in which soldiers used tanks long before the tank was so much as a blue-print in the War Office.) Shaw was interested in what the men themselves would have become. So in his plays about the future the background is always negligible and it is the views and conversation of the human beings themselves which matter. But Shaw wanted to indicate that the Longlivers had discovered some power strong enough to check aggression, otherwise evolutionary longevity would always be prevented by war. (He was writing just after the 1914–18 war when the massacre of the young men of Europe was very much in his mind.) Bulwer-Lytton, who had written a novel of future-fiction in 1871, when Darwinism was in its first spate of enthusiasm, had also visualized the men of the future having a power of this kind. In his book, *The Coming Race* (in which everyone had wings, and women were the dominant sex), he had called it Vril. By Vril the Coming Race struck aggressors dead merely by giving them a magnetic stare. Shaw—who was extremely earnest about his theme—wanted to suggest some power which was already latent in human beings and which really could develop in this way, by evolution. He remembered that when he was in his early twenties he had had a few minutes' conversation with an aged Jewish Rabbi and had been completely overawed by him, and reduced to a subjection which he had never experienced before and never did again. "I was simply discouraged by him," he said. Primitive tribes are said to have the same sensation at the impact of civilized invaders. Shaw decided from this example that every living person has a magnetic field of greater or less intensity which enables those in whom it is strong to dominate those in whom it is relatively weak. In *Back to Methuselah*, the Longlivers have developed it in themselves to such an extent that it is dangerous to their visitors. They have to make regulations for the protection of tourists. One Longliver warns a tourist that he is not observing the regulations laid down for shortlived people.

THE WOMAN (*severely*). They apply to you very strictly. You are expected to confine yourself to the society of children under sixty. You are absolutely forbidden to approach fully adult natives under any circumstances. You cannot converse with persons of my age for long without bringing on a dangerous attack of discouragement. Do you realize that you are already showing signs of that very distressing and usually fatal complaint?

Just as all writers find it difficult to make goodness attractive, so those who write about the supermen of a super-civilized future find it almost impossible to make them either credible or as admirable as they aim to. Shaw was no exception. He concentrates on presenting his Longlivers as supremely calm and rational. One critic described them as "Shavian super-prigs". They treat their tourist-worshippers with irritable patronage.

ZOO. Why do you shortlivers persist in making up silly stories about the world, and trying to act as if they were true? Contact with truth hurts and frightens you: you escape from it into an imaginary vacuum in which you can indulge your desires and hopes and loves and hates without any obstruction from the solid facts of life. You love to throw dust in your own eyes.

In this Utopia of Shaw's imagination, some of his own favourite schemes for the ideal socialist state have become common usage. Motherhood is treated as an honourable profession, a service to the state, and all mothers have long ago conquered all personal possessiveness about their children. One of the Longlivers, a young woman (of fifty-six) who is looking after an elderly tourist, carelessly refers to her babies.

THE ELDERLY GENTLEMAN. Your babies!!! I fear I am treading on very delicate ground; but your appearance is extremely youthful; and if I may ask how many——?

ZOO. Only four as yet. It is a long business with us. I specialize in babies. My first was such a success that they made me go on.

Later, the elderly gentleman refers sentimentally to his own old mother.

ZOO. Do you mean to say that your mother bothered about you after you were ten?

THE ELDERLY GENTLEMAN. Naturally, madam. She was my mother. What would you have had her to do?

ZOO. Go on to the next, of course. After eight or nine, children become quite uninteresting, except to themselves. I shouldnt know my two eldest if I met them.

From the very first, the Longlivers have grown out of the Shortlivers' obsession about sex. In the 2170 A.D. scene one of the ordinary mortals has mentioned marriage to the longliving ex-parlourmaid. He is severely snubbed.

THE ARCHBISHOP. Can you shortlived people not understand that as the confusion and immaturity and primitive animalism in which we live for the first hundred years of our life is worse in this matter of sex than in any other, you are intolerable to us in that relation?

By the year 31,920 A.D. the human species has evolved so far that it has succeeded in condensing all human emotionalism into a brief four-year span of first youth. Children now go through the whole period of childhood (which Shaw found so tiresome) inside an egg, are born fully-grown and allowed to survive if perfect. They then have their human "childhood" in which to try out and exhaust the pleasures of the senses. A She-Ancient (or fully adult person) explains the process to a newly-born one.

THE SHE-ANCIENT. Now listen. You have four years of childhood before you. You will not be very happy: but you will be interested and amused by the novelty of the world: and your companions here will teach you how to keep up an imitation of happiness during your four years, by what they call arts and sports and pleasures.

When the children are young they dread growing up and becoming Ancients themselves, and talk of putting an end to their lives when the four years are almost up. But as they come nearer to being adult they find they are becoming bored by youthful pursuits and that they stay awake to meditate instead of sleeping all night as they used to.

MARTELLUS. Well, I have finished with the dolls: and I am no longer jealous of you. That looks like the end. Two hours sleep is enough for me. I am afraid I am beginning to find you all rather silly.
STREPHON. I know. My girl went off this morning. She hadnt slept for weeks. And she found mathematics more interesting than me.

The Ancients, at first, interest themselves in evolutionary experiments. One wills herself into growing extra legs and arms. But one day as she sits with her four chins resting on her four palms and her four elbows on her four knees she realizes that there is no object in making her body into an automaton and enslaving it. In the end, all Ancients give up all follies of the kind and wander about, alone, from century to century, in meditation, that is living the life of the mind fully and completely, and doing nothing else. They have discovered how to conquer ordinary physical decay of the body, but they know that some day each individual Ancient will inevitably meet a fatal accident. Meanwhile they have one trouble; the tyranny of being imprisoned in a body at all.

THE HE-ANCIENT. That, children, is the trouble of the ancients. For whilst we are tied to this tyrannous body we are subject to its death and our destiny is not achieved.

THE NEWLY-BORN. What is your destiny?

THE HE-ANCIENT. To be immortal.

THE SHE-ANCIENT. The day will come when there will be no people, only thought.

The play ends with a dream-scene in which the ghosts of Adam and Eve, who first launched the human race, ask each other what it has all been for. Lilith, the eternal mother, who came even before them, prophesies a future in which "these infants who call themselves Ancients" will develop into something that is "all life and no matter". She cannot tell what they will be. "It is enough that there is a beyond."

# 13 About a New Alphabet

Shaw said "The English have no respect for their language and will not teach their children to speak it. . . . It is impossible for an Englishman to open his mouth without making some other Englishman despise him."

This is part of the class-consciousness perpetuated by the British education system, in which you acquire an accent which will identify you by class for ever after. But it works both ways. The Etonian learns to despise those without an Etonian accent. But the working man who despises gentlemanly parasites guards against being confused with them. In *Man and Superman*, the hero always introduces his chauffeur as "Mr Enry Straker" because, "This man takes more trouble to drop his aitches than ever his father did to pick them up. It's a mark of caste to him. I have never met anybody more swollen with the pride of class than Enry is."

The reason for the difference of accents in the first place is because the English alphabet has not enough vowels in it to express the different sounds of the language. Even when you use combinations of vowels there is no general agreement about the pronunciation, and not all of the consonants have any agreed speech value. Therefore it is impossible to teach yourself what the language should sound like from reading it, and so the speech of the English is slipshod, ugly and incomprehensible. Shaw wrote *Pygmalion* to illustrate his argument that we need a phonetic alphabet. It delighted him that a subject which sounded so dry and didactic should turn out to be the most popular of all his plays. In the play, Professor Higgins, a phonetics expert, transforms a Cockney flower-girl into a society lady by teaching her to speak beautifully.

HIGGINS. A woman who utters such depressing and disgusting sounds has no right to be anywhere—no right to live. Remember that you are a human being with a soul and the divine gift of articulate speech: that your native language is the language of Shakespeare and Milton and the Bible: and dont sit there crooning like a bilious pigeon.

ELIZA (*quite overwhelmed, looking up at him in mingled wonder and deprecation without daring to raise her head*). Ah-ah-ah-ow-ow-ow-oo!

HIGGINS (*whipping out his book*). Heavens! What a sound! (*He writes, then holds out the book and reads, reproducing her vowels exactly*). Ah-ah-ah-ow-ow-ow-oo!

ELIZA (*tickled by the performance and laughing in spite of herself*). Garn!

HIGGINS. You see this creature with her kerbstone English: the English that will keep her in the gutter to the end of her days. Well, sir, in three months I could pass that girl off as a duchess at an ambassador's garden party. I could even get her a place as a lady's maid or shop assistant which requires better English.

Shaw's most-quoted line of all occurs in this play, at the point where Eliza is half-way through her re-education. She can now articulate perfectly and pronounce every word correctly. But her language and the content of her conversation still belong to her East-End background. Higgins tries her out by sending her to make a formal call in a Kensington drawing-room. She manages to talk and behave well enough to pass as a lady until the last moment, when an infatuated young man is seeing her out.

FREDDY (*opening the door for her*). Are you walking across the Park, Miss Doolittle? If so——
ELIZA (*with perfectly elegant diction*). Walk? Not bloody likely. (*Sensation*). I am going in a taxi.

In 1913, this line caused a tremendous furore. Audiences were delightedly shocked, and the press wrote about it for a whole week. Shaw said afterwards that although he had been writing seriously about the coming war and how it could be avoided, for years before, no one had taken any notice, but that this one word made him instantly famous, beyond the Kaiser, the Tsar, Shakespeare and Homer and President Wilson. By the time *Pygmalion* became *My Fair Lady* "bloody" had become allowable. It was regarded as only slightly blasphemous slang among educated and uneducated people alike, either because the social climate had become less strict, or because Shaw's line had become a catch-phrase and so familiar. The script-writers of the musical version thought it no longer carried the joke it was meant to, and substituted a line in which Eliza refers to a "ruddy arse". But (like most re-written jokes) it missed the mark.

In his earlier plays, when Shaw wanted to convey the particular pronunciation of any character, he spelt the words out phonetically, a habit which makes parts of the plays tiresome to read. An American is always presented as saying "dullicate" for delicate. In *John Bull's Other Island* he conveys an Irish brogue by writing out "dhat" for that, "Prodestan" for Protestant, "hwat" for what and so on. In *Major Barbara* he wants to reproduce Cockney speech: "Wot prawce selvytion nah?" But it took him a long time, and Shaw was impatient. He had begun his career as a public speaker and always found writing slow after it. He thought, as he said, in dialogue, and so his thought outran the speed of his pen. Because of this he learned shorthand and kept it up so that even after ninety he could still compose fifteen hundred words a day.

He had some private foibles of his own about the appearance of his printed work. He refused to use the apostrophe in such colloquial phrases as "can't" and "don't", writing them as "cant" and "dont" instead. He disliked commas. He said that the Bible would never have attained its supreme position in literature if it had been disfigured with such unsightly signs.

After he had met Henry Sweet, an eccentric phonetics expert from Oxford—and the original of Professor Higgins in the play—Shaw began to work out the idea of a new British alphabet which would transform the language and save time in writing it. The Proposed British Alphabet was to have at least forty letters. Even so, said Shaw, it would not pretend to be exhaustive. "It contains only sixteen vowels whereas by infinitesimal movements of the tongue countless different vowels can be produced, all of them in use among speakers of English who utter the same vowels no oftener than they make the same fingerprints. Nevertheless they can understand one another's speech and writing sufficiently to converse and correspond: for instance, a graduate of Trinity College Dublin has no difficulty in understanding a graduate of Oxford university when one says that 'the sun rohze' and the other that 'the sun raheoze' nor are either of them puzzled when a peasant calls his childhood his 'chawldid'. For a university graduate calls my native country 'Awlind.'" Shaw suggested that the letter "O" should have different vowel-signs for its various pronunciations in "on", "oak", "out", "wool" and "ooze". Consonants should be rationalized, with different signs for "th" as in "thigh", "they", and different signs again for "su" according to whether it was pronounced as in "measure" or in "sure".

In his old age Shaw became more and more interested in the idea of the foundation of a new alphabet and left a part of his money to establish a fund to get it launched. He directed his trustees to arrange for research and reports and for a model set of signs to be drawn up. As a basic pronunciation, they were to take "that recorded of His Majesty our late King George V and sometimes described as Northern English". When the form of the alphabet had been finally agreed upon Shaw ordered that an expert was then to translate *Androcles and the Lion* into it, and that the play was to be published with the ordinary version and on each opposite page its facsimile in the Proposed British Alphabet. These instructions of

Shaw's have now been carried out and you can find the
*Shaw Alphabet Edition of Androcles and the Lion* in any
public library, looking like this:

ᚱᚱᚱᚱᚱᚱᚱ. ᚱᚱ ᚱᚱ ᚱ ᚱᚱᚱᚱᚱ, ᚱᚱ: ᚱ ᚱᚱ ᚱ ᚱᚱᚱᚱ.

ᚱᚱᚱᚱ. ᚱᚱ, ᚱᚱᚱ ᚱᚱᚱ ᚱ ᚱᚱᚱ ᚱᚱᚱ, ᚱᚱᚱ ᚱᚱ ᚱᚱᚱ ᚱᚱᚱ?

# 14 Summary of Shaw's Best-Known Works

Mrs Warren's Profession.
Arms and the Man.
Candida.
The Man of Destiny.
You Never Can Tell.
The Devil's Disciple.
Caesar and Cleopatra.
Man and Superman.
John Bull's Other Island.
Major Barbara.
The Doctor's Dilemma.
Androcles and the Lion.
Pygmalion.
Heartbreak House.

Back to Methuselah.
Saint Joan.
The Apple-Cart.
The Intelligent Woman's Guide to Socialism.
The Black Girl In Search of God.
Everybody's Political What's What.

### Mrs Warren's Profession

This is a play about a successful university girl, Vivie
Warren, who learns that her education and the wealthy
background in which she has been brought up were all
paid for by money earned by prostitutes. Her mother,
Mrs Warren, began her life in the most desperate poverty
and took to prostitution because it was the only way in
which she could earn more than a pittance. She had
great business ability and determination and in time
owned a chain of brothels. This enabled her to give her
own daughter every possible advantage.

Mrs Warren, in a powerful and moving scene, justifies
the life she had led and Vivie admits that she cannot blame
her. But Vivie only takes in the full significance of the
story when she realises that she is herself illegitimate and
that the parson's son, with whom she is having a light-
hearted love affair, is her half-brother. Vivie is made of
the same hard, realistic metal as her mother. She does
not pass moral judgment on her, but she leaves her finally
because Mrs Warren would be a liability in the life she
wishes to lead.

This play, written in 1894, was privately produced in
London in 1902 and publicly in New York in 1905. The
cast was arrested, on a charge of "disorderly conduct".

The outcry it caused was not because of any indecency

in the dialogue but because the subject of prostitution was, for the first time on the stage, treated coldly and realistically without the conventional sentimental trappings. Shaw wrote it when he was much under the influence of Ibsen, but it is more brisk and cheerful than Ibsen's *Ghosts* on the same kind of theme.

A much-quoted line which sums it up is—"What is any respectable girl brought up to do but to catch some rich man's fancy and get the benefit of his money by marrying him?—as if a marriage ceremony could make any difference in the right or the wrong of the thing!"

### *Arms and the Man*

This is a gay comedy about war set during a Balkan war which had happened nine years before Shaw wrote it. It is about the contrast between a romantic and dashing war hero and a strong-minded and drily practical professional soldier. The first act in which the realist professional—on the run from the victorious army of the other side—breaks into the heroine's bedroom is one of the most brilliantly written first acts in English comedy. The play ends with the heroine marrying him and the romantic one bestowing his name and fortune on her pert little maid.

It was produced in 1894 and after a doubtful start became one of the classics of the English stage. Later an operatic version of it was made, with music by Oscar Strauss—*The Chocolate Soldier*. Shaw wrote this also under Ibsen's influence, with naturalism and realism. It mocks romanticism, but only with laughter, without exposure of terrible truths. All the same, it shocked audiences by making fun of cherished ideals, such as military heroism, high-minded love-affairs and the glory of small nations fighting for nationalist freedom. The most-quoted line is:

"What use are cartridges in battle? I always carry chocolate instead."

### Candida

This is about the reality behind an ideal home. The Reverend James Morell is a Christian Socialist parson, a reformer and popular preacher, beloved by his colleagues, with a happy family life and a wife, Candida, to whom he is devoted. One of his protégés, an aristocratic young poet, Marchbanks, falls in love with Candida. At first Morell genially laughs it off but Marchbanks punctures his self-esteem and Morell is driven to asking Candida to choose between them. Candida is irritated that Morell cannot see further than his own image of himself as her master and protector or beyond his own limited vision of love. If she had to give what she calls her purity, rather than let Marchbanks become degraded by learning about love from the wrong woman, she would do it as readily as she would give her shawl to save him from cold. Like Ibsen's heroine of *A Doll's House* she has her own soul. She stays with her husband not because of his strength but because he is weaker than Marchbanks. The poet can follow his destiny on his own.

*Candida* was first produced in Durham in 1895 and five years later in London, with Ellen Terry in the title-role. It had a bigger success in New York. Not all of Shaw's critics liked it. His fellow-Fabian, Beatrice Webb, saw it merely as the story of a middle-aged wife in search of extra-marital romance. (But perhaps she was irritated because she thought Morell was modelled on the Fabians.)

This is one of the few plays Shaw wrote which are about personalities rather than issues. Candida is the ideal mother-figure of the stage. Of all Shaw's plays this is the one which has made most audiences cry.

The most-quoted lines:

"It is easy—terribly easy—to shake a man's faith in himself. To take advantage of that to break a man's spirit is devil's work."

### The Man of Destiny

This is a short play about an imaginary incident in the life of Napoleon. It has a deliberately charming heroine because Shaw wrote it specially for Ellen Terry at the time when his long-distance romantic affair with her was at its height. Shaw told Ellen Terry that this was not one of his best plays but a commercial traveller's sample of stage tricks. It is about the young Napoleon and the plot hangs on the story of a disguised lady and some stolen dispatches. It succeeded and lives on because of its witty dialogue. It was Shaw's first historical play and it surprised and intrigued the public by breaking away from the traditional "period" dialogue and by treating historical characters as though they had been contemporary people, talking and acting in an ordinary modern way. It started the fashion for natural plays set in the past. The most-quoted lines in it are those in which Napoleon gives a long description of the English character, beginning with "The English are a nation of shopkeepers".

### You Never Can Tell

Shaw wrote this play deliberately to be a commercial success. West-End managers wanted a comedy with fun, fashionable dresses, music, eating and drinking in stylish surroundings, love-scenes, family tangles and a comic waiter. Shaw supplied them all and added a Shakespearean-type title. But he also managed to slip in a little light-hearted discussion of social problems; such as the relationship between parents and children and the conflict between the intellectual ideal of rational love and the reality of physical attraction. He wrote it at the time when he was falling in love with his future wife and it is one of his happiest plays. The most original part of it is the introduction of a lively and attractive brother and sister, seventeen years old, who have just arrived in England and are gay and irrepressible and continually outraging English sedateness. (The idea caught on, and has been copied by other dramatists since.) Shaw's twins laugh at their intellectual sister's series of admirers and in particular at their new dentist who falls in love with her at first sight. They ask the dentist and his landlord to lunch, where it turns out that the landlord is their father, who has been separated from their mother since they were babies. The play is occupied with the differences between their progressive and feminist mother and their surly father, the family breach being eventually settled by an eminent barrister who turns out to be the son of the hotel waiter. The charm of this light comedy is the speed and sparkle of the dialogue and the neatness with which the situations are contrived and handled. It was first produced in 1899.

The most-quoted line—the title.

### The Devil's Disciple

This was written by Shaw as a melodrama suitable for the world tour of a popular actor. Today it would be described as a light-hearted thriller but it raises deeper issues than the average thriller. It was Shaw's version of the nineteenth-century fashion of having an anti-hero, rebelling against the Old Testament God. It is set during the American War of Independence and is the story of a bad man who against his will develops what Shaw called moral passion. He sets himself up as the devil's disciple, but when it comes to the point of crisis in his life he finds himself deliberately going to the gallows to save another man. The other man, a Christian minister who thought that he was a pacifist, finds himself constitutionally unable to keep that up. He takes off his black coat, gives up his living and joins the Resistance against the occupying British. The minister's wife falls in love with the hero, but only to enable Shaw to emphasize that he is not in love with her; that he did not do his good deed for romantic love but for moral passion.

*The Devil's Disciple* was first performed in America in 1897 and two years later in England. It has been successfully revived many times since and was made into a film in 1959. The most-quoted point in it is the one about the minister who was honest enough to resign from the church when he found he was no longer able to subscribe to the New Testament ideal of turning the other cheek and loving your enemies. In 1914 Shaw bitterly recommended his example to the English clergy who were whipping up anti-German hysteria from their pulpits.

### Caesar and Cleopatra

Shaw was inspired to write this play by the publication of a biography of Julius Caesar based on the work of a German scholar, Mommsen. It is a series of engaging sketches rather than a single drama. It imagines Caesar at the height of his career, before the time described by Shakespeare—his downfall and assassination. Caesar was having a love-affair (according to rumour) with the young and fascinatingly clever Queen Cleopatra of Egypt. Shaw, like Mommsen, assumes that it was not a serious one and that Caesar simply found her youthful charm engaging. Early in the play Caesar comes on Cleopatra in the desert. She has run away from her palace, terrified of the impending arrival of the Roman general. Caesar persuades her that she must be brave and face him, which she prepares to do, only to find that the old gentleman who has befriended her is the mighty general himself.

What matters most in this play is the contrast between the really great man and the pettiness, malice and spite of the others compared with him. Shaw's Caesar is one of the most vivid and lovable characters of the English stage. He is, perhaps, what Shaw would have been in Caesar's shoes, a man loftily above common meannesses, knowing and accepting his own unimportant weaknesses, merciful by preference, kind by nature, ruled by rational judgment and not emotion, killing when necessary without moralizing or hypocrisy, seeing further than other men, humorous and sweet-tempered because he has no doubts of himself; a leader of men to be admired and adored. Shaw said that he wrote the play to show how Shakespeare really ought to have done it and to provide a philosopher-hero part for the actor Forbes-Robertson. It was first produced in America and Germany and in England in 1906. One critic called it the story of *The Funny Old Gentleman and the Silly Little Girl*. It has always been one of the most-loved of Shaw's plays, although it is not often performed, probably because it is expensive to put on. It was filmed in 1945. Shaw was moderately pleased with the film, though it does not give the real heart of the play, but tends to concentrate on large-scale crowd scenes, whereas the real drama and suspense and development of character depend on small scenes and economical dialogue. The most-quoted line is probably Caesar's description of his British slave: "He is a barbarian and thinks that the customs of his tribe and island are the laws of nature."

### Man and Superman

Shaw wrote this after the dramatic critic of *The Times* had challenged him to write a Don Juan or love-play. It took him three years to write. It is generally considered one of his best plays.

In it, he turns the conventional formula of the love-play —boy meets girl, boy loses girl, boy gets girl—upside down. Shaw's version is girl meets boy, loses boy, gets boy. This reversal is important because all the way through his plays this is Shaw's version of sexual love. It shook the public considerably, because before this Romance—at least after Shakespeare's time—had been the story of the man hunting down the reluctant but finally yielding woman. Shaw's formula was the basis of his philosophy of the Life Force. What people call Love, he said, is a trick of nature to ensure the continuance of the race and its improvement through evolution. It is the most powerful emotion because it is the Life Force's chief vehicle for carrying out its plan. In 1905 this matter-of-fact stripping away of romance from a love-story was far more revolutionary than the "dust-bin" school of play-writing was to audiences of the nineteen-sixties.

The pattern of the play is unusual, because in the middle of it there is a long dream-sequence—"Don Juan in Hell"—in which the hero dreams that he is Don Juan and has gone to hell because he would not fulfil the purpose of the Life Force which (for him) was to father the Superman. Hell is the home of the seekers for happiness. There are no social questions or political or religious ones. Everything is amusement and amateurism. Its inmates could go to heaven any time they like, but they prefer to stay where they are for heaven means facing reality. The main story is complete without this act, and the play is usually performed without it, because otherwise it is abnormally long. But this does mean that Shaw's own exposition of his Life Force theory is lost and also that the audience loses one of the most outstanding pieces of rhetorical dialogue written for the twentieth-century stage.

The main play is a sparkling comedy of social life, about a determined young woman who sets out to get an intellectual man as a husband and the father of her children. The man, Tanner, is a revolutionary who has freed himself from the social conventions of his circle, and the comedy is in his trying to escape and in the girl catching him without infringing the rules. The book which Tanner is supposed to have written, *The Revolutionist's Handbook*, consisting of controversial maxims, is part of the published version of the play. Tanner is more identified with Shaw himself than any other creation of Shaw's.

Shaw's theme that an intellectual man and a beautiful woman of strong personality were fit parents for the Superman inspired an unknown woman to write to him saying that as he had the greatest brain in the world and she the most beautiful body they ought to get together and produce the perfect child. Shaw replied, "What if the child inherits my beauty and your brains?"

*Man and Superman* was written between 1901 and 1903 and first produced in 1905 but without the hell scene, though that was done separately in 1907. The complete play was first produced in 1915. It is generally counted as one of the classics of the English stage. Many of the "maxims for revolutionists" are Shaw's most-quoted sayings, but a much-quoted one from the play itself is: "A lifetime of happiness: no man alive could bear it; it would be hell on earth."

### John Bull's Other Island

This play, written and produced in 1904, was one of the Royal Court Theatre's most successful ventures of all time. The Prime Minister saw it four times, and there was a Royal Command performance. When it was first put on audiences used to laugh so much that leaflets had to be distributed asking them not to slow down the pace by laughing too much and too long. It was written at a time when the question whether Ireland should or should not have Home Rule was one of the most argued topics of the day. John Bull's "other island" is, of course, Ireland. In the play a bumbling Gladstonian Liberal is sure that he can do right by the Irish, and teach them to be efficient whilst preserving their Celtic charm. The Irish flatter him to his face and laugh uncontrollably at him behind his back. The most-remembered character of all in this play is Father Keegan, a priest-mystic who is contrasted with the authoritative regular priest, part of the powerful

Catholic Church establishment of Ireland. The line which best sums up the play is, "There are only two qualities in the world, efficiency and inefficiency: and only two sorts of people: the efficient and the inefficient."

## Major Barbara

This is Shaw's play about the Salvation Army, but what he is discussing is whether it is possible to restore a man's self-respect and identity—to save his soul—without eliminating his poverty first. Shaw is quite certain that it is poverty which destroys a man. It is the story of an armaments millionaire who convinces his daughter that he "saves" men and women, by good wages, housing and working conditions more effectively than she can through the Salvation Army. It was written and produced in 1905 and has been steadily successful, though audiences have always liked the first part more than the end. It is often revived and was filmed in 1941. Shaw liked and admired the Salvation Army and had defended their music against critics, which was what first gave him the idea of writing this play. The most often-remembered line is the armament-manufacturer's: "Poverty is the worst of crimes."

## The Doctor's Dilemma

The dilemma of the doctor-hero is whether he should use his power of life and death to enforce a moral judgment. He has discovered a successful cure for TB, but can only offer it to a limited number of patients and has to choose between a dull, ineffective fellow-doctor who will never do much good or harm in the world and a really gifted artist whose work will enrich it. The issue is complicated by the doctor falling in love with the artist's wife and wishing she was free to marry him. But it is decided by the doctor's discovery that the artist is a conscienceless scoundrel. The doctor leaves the artist to the care of a distinguished but careless and ignorant colleague whose treatment he believes will kill the patient.

Though this play is remembered for its comedy, in the exposure of medical practice as Shaw saw it, his theme was a serious one—the responsibility of the medical scientist, and the irresponsibility forced on the doctor by being paid fees, instead of drawing a salary from the state. It was written forty years before the foundation of the National Health Service.

The indefensible scoundrel artist of this play was based on the character and life-story of a real man, an acquaintance of Shaw's who seduced Karl Marx's daughter and deserted her, after which she committed suicide. Most of the doctors in the play were portraits of real-life ones of the time. Their real names have long been forgotten, but the play-characters have given them an anonymous immortality.

"All professions are conspiracies against the laity."

### Androcles and the Lion

There was a vogue for melodramas about Christian martyrs going to the arena in the Edwardian theatre. They ran to a set pattern with stock characters. This was Shaw's parody of the pattern but he was in earnest about his Christians. He achieved the almost incredible feat of making it a very funny comedy while respecting the faith and courage of his martyrs. The critics called it "a religious pantomime".

It was written and produced in 1912. Shaw went to rehearsals and insisted on its being done in his own way. It was a commercial success but there was a storm of criticism about its alleged blasphemy. The religious press raged against it. Shaw persisted that it was a religious drama with comic relief. Probably no play about religion since the Mystery Plays of the church itself (which also had comic relief) has so clearly put the issues of Christianity before the ordinary public. They had to listen, because of the brilliance of the dialogue and the skill of the dramatic situations. Shaw's philosophy in it is passionate and sincere. Lavinia, the fearless free-thinking Christian, has most in common with his own personal faith.

The Emperor of the play is a silly-clever Prussian-type popular idol. When the Crown Prince of Germany went to see it he walked out of the theatre as a protest against the portrayal. Shaw commented that he was glad the German Emperor's son had understood the significance so well, but that the Empire he was really thinking of was nearer home.

Many people think that this is Shaw's most valuable play. It was made into a film in 1955, but the producer missed the point and made it into a commonplace love-story between Lavinia and the Roman captain of the play.

"It is since all the stories and dreams have gone that I have now no doubt at all that I must die for something greater than dreams or stories."

## *Pygmalion*

The professor of phonetics makes a society lady out of a Cockney girl by teaching her to speak beautifully.

Professor Higgins is an expert who can distinguish 130 different vowel-sounds in spoken English and can tell, by a person's speech, exactly which district of the British Isles is his home-town. He takes on the experiment of training Eliza, the flower-girl, as a bet with a fellow-scholar. Alfred Doolittle, Eliza's father, tries to blackmail Higgins, but Higgins completely defeats him and Doolittle eventually becomes a pillar of middle-class morality. Eliza's re-education, after some threatened disasters, succeeds in weaning her away completely from her background. But where is she to go next? She now belongs nowhere.

Shaw wrote the role of Eliza for Mrs. Patrick Campbell, a famous and temperamental actress of the time, with whom he was half-seriously in love. It was written just before the 1914 war and first produced in Vienna, then in England. It was Shaw's *As You Like It*, the eternal Cinderella story, full of witty lines, all the characters pure comedy but credible and likeable. Quotations from it have become part of the language—notably "middle-class morality" and "not bloody likely". It has been revived over and over again all over the world, was successfully filmed in 1938 and set to music as *My Fair Lady* in 1956, since when it has had a phenomenal success on both sides of the Atlantic. *My Fair Lady* itself was filmed in 1964.

### Heartbreak House

Shaw wrote this play in semi-retirement during the 1914–18 war. It is his first play in surrealist style—that is like a dream—and the dramatic pattern is Tchekovian—a group of people in a country house and their impact on each other.

The house of the title is an English country-house without its real centre—the stables—and the inhabitants have therefore degenerated into a pointless Bohemianism. It stands for Shaw's picture of pre-1914 England, no longer "Horseback Hall", the England of the squirearchy, but without a substitute set of ideals or way of life. The characters are the types of the period—the old sailor, the mem-Sahib, the worthless younger brother of the Empire-builder, the upper-class idler, the ineffective radical, the business tycoon and the young lady who has got to marry a man she does not love because there is no other way of getting herself new gloves. They all lament their own boredom and lack of direction but have not the intelligence or purpose to change. An air-raid—representing the war—comes as a welcome relief to them. It was produced in New York in 1920 and in London in 1921. It was received respectfully by critics and public though not with anything like the enthusiasm there had been for *Pygmalion*. It is revived from time to time by serious repertory companies, and audiences are usually surprised to find how amused and entertained they are, without necessarily associating the story with its original theme.

Shaw thought well of this play himself. It is different from all his others because of its leisured melancholy pace. It was written when he himself felt mournful and hopeless. But in his puppet play about himself and Shakespeare, he makes the puppet "Shav" quote from *Heartbreak House* to prove that he can write as good tragic verse as *King Lear*. The air-raid which winds up the play was inspired by a Zeppelin incident near his own home, and the burglar who breaks into Heartbreak House and outwits the residents of it was based on a burglar who broke into Shaw's London flat. If there is a character identified with Shaw himself in the play, it is the eccentric old Captain Shotover who continually dashes in and out, giving wild paradoxical advice to the uneasy residents. None of them take it.

"Do you think the laws of God will be suspended in favour of England because you were born in it?"

### Back to Methuselah

This was Shaw's confession of faith as a Creative Evolutionist. He thought it his greatest work. It begins in the garden of Eden and ends in the unforeseeable future. Between the two, Shaw explains his belief that man cannot progress and improve unless he learns to live longer.

In the garden of Eden, Adam and Eve cannot endure the thought of living for ever, but death is too terrible an alternative. The Serpent tells Eve that there is a way out. Man can renew himself, in birth. They try it, but when their sons are born, Cain is a killer, the military man whose only outlet is destruction, and who shortens man's lifespan for the whole human race.

Ages later, in the nineteen-twenties, after the military man has had his greatest-ever holocaust, two scholars discover that man could live as long as he pleased if only his will to do so was strong enough. Two politicians consider using the idea as an election slogan. The scholars, discouraged by the frivolity and disbelief with which they are met, give up hope of convincing anyone. But in the next part, two and a half centuries later, two of the nineteen-twenties' characters—the local curate and the scholars' parlourmaid—are still alive though they do not know each other. Everyone fears and reveres them, without knowing why. The reason is that these two are the only fully adult characters among ordinary people, who are childish compared with them. They discover each other by chance and decide, quite rationally and cold-bloodedly, that they must get married to each other to produce a longlived race.

In the next part it is 3000 A.D. The Longlivers are a separate race and culture living in the west of Ireland. Visitors go to them in order to have their minds made flexible and to consult the oracle. An elderly gentleman, part of a conducted tour, is so impressed by their lofty wisdom that he cannot endure the thought of going back to his own superficial civilization. He is permitted to die instantly instead.

In the final instalment—31920 A.D.—the Longlivers have taken over the world. Children are now born, fully grown, from eggs. Human beings die only from a fatal accident which, although it may not happen for centuries, is bound to overtake each one eventually. When the children reach adulthood they lose interest in trivialities and the concerns of the flesh and spend their time in intellectual meditation and mental ecstasy. All they want now is to find a way of dispensing with the machinery of the body altogether.

There is an epilogue in which Lilith, the original mother, reflects that life is still developing, man still reaching out towards the future, and that one day her seed will master the universe.

*Back to Methuselah* was written between 1918–21, produced in New York in three separate parts in 1922, and in England in 1923 with the five acts as five separate performances. It is too long to be done on a single occasion and is a risk for a producer because of the cost of putting on an epic on this scale. Barry Jackson took the risk, from loyalty to Shaw, but Shaw warned him to make certain his wife and children were provided for first. It was important to Shaw because it summed up the theology of his own invention.

"We die in boyhood: the maturity that should make us the greatest of all the nations lies beyond the grave for us."

### Saint Joan

There is general agreement that this is Shaw's masterpiece. Many people think it the greatest play of the twentieth century.

Shaw wrote it in consequence of a tactful suggestion from his wife. In 1920 Joan of Arc was canonized; that is, the Catholic church decided that the "voices" which directed her, and for which the church excommunicated her and handed her over to the English, who burned her alive, really had come from God. When the canonization was announced, there was a spate of new books and histories about her. Mrs. Shaw left some of them lying about the house at Ayot St. Lawrence in the hope that Shaw would pick them up and become interested and decide to write a play about Joan. He did.

Joan of Arc was a village girl who led the French resistance against the occupying British army in the early fifteenth century, was captured, judged a heretic and executed. Shaw saw her as the first protestant and the first nationalist and as a military genius and saint.

The early scenes of the play, written in a swift and exciting style, show how Joan first persuaded the local squire, who in mediaeval days was also the local military commander, to help her in what she saw as her divine

mission to drive the English out of France; how she persuaded the Court and the uncrowned Dauphin to accept
her; and how she won a victory which drove the English
back and led to the crowning of the Dauphin as the
rightful king of France. But the powers which stood for
the security and stability of the Middle Ages, the feudal
barons and the Church, conspire against her. The feudal
lords are represented by the English Earl of Warwick, a
strong-willed and able politician and soldier, a smooth and
cultured aristocrat. The church is represented by the
Bishop of Beauvais, a completely sincere but conventional
priest. Joan, as an individualist, a protestant, and a
nationalist stands for forces which were throwing over the
old order and is therefore a dangerous revolutionary and
heretic. Warwick and the Bishop agree to capture her and
bring her to trial for heresy. Her friends at the French
court prove too weak and vacillating to prevent it. Joan is
found guilty and confesses to heresy. But when she learns
that she is to be condemned to perpetual imprisonment
she prefers to die, recants her confession and is burned at
the stake. An English chaplain, who as a jingo Englishman
has struggled for her conviction and execution, is overcome
by remorse when he sees her burned and is driven insane.

Twenty-five years later Joan returns to the king in a
dream and learns that the sentence of heresy on her has
been annulled and the English have been driven from
France. In the ghost-world she meets again the characters
of her short period of dynamic fame. Among them
appears a Vatican official of 1920 to tell them that Joan is
to be made a saint. She offers to return to life if they will
have her, but one and all refuse. Joan is left alone,
deserted but spiritually triumphant.

The construction of the play is probably as near to perfection as any drama in English literature. If you examine the skeleton of the play-story you find that it follows the traditional pattern of a Greek tragedy. This began with the struggle of the hero against his enemies, then recounted his destruction or tearing to pieces; continued with the lament for his death and his triumph in glory, and ended with his resurrection. The play *Saint Joan* fits into this pattern like the pieces of a jig-saw puzzle.

Joan the maid is the noblest character in all Shaw's work. But there are no evil characters in this play; the tragedy is the conflict of belief against belief. The long dialogues in which Warwick puts the point of view of feudalism against the nationalist and the Bishop that of the church against the heretic are the most dramatic arguments Shaw ever wrote.

By the time he wrote it he had freed himself from the influence of Ibsen. In this subject there was no scope for Socialism, no social problems to discuss, no private prejudices to be aired, nor opportunity to illustrate Creative Evolution. There was only the story of a real girl, long ago, who stood out against the might of feudal Europe and the Catholic church, alone, guided only by her inner light; a story about human beings and God. It was the peak of Shaw's work. He had never written anything as good, and he never did again.

"O God that madest this beautiful earth, when will it be ready to receive Thy saints? How long, O Lord, how long?"

### The Apple-Cart

This is a satirical play about British politics, set in the

future. Shaw wrote it seven years after *Saint Joan*. It was the longest gap in his playwriting career, because he had been writing his testament of Socialism in between. He returned to drama with this play because Barry Jackson had asked him to provide one to open the Malvern Festival which first began in the summer of 1929. Inevitably, it was a descent from *Saint Joan*. Shaw said it was a bag of stage tricks, as old as Sophocles. But they still work. *The Apple-Cart* has the speed and wit and lucidity of the best of his plays. It is always good entertainment.

It is also good argument. In his book about Socialism, Shaw had been busy summarizing his views about society and democracy in the simplest possible language. When he followed it with this play, he illustrated his view of democratic government by a story in which a philosopher-king completely outwits his own cabinet, because, said Shaw, "one man who has a mind and knows it can always beat ten who havnt and dont".

The king who upsets the apple-cart of democracy does it because he is now the only individual who can stand between the masses and their bosses. The elected government would not dare to be tyrannical. But the vested interests really dictate to the government and the country. Only the king can still afford to stand and to fight for the great abstractions.

The story which carries the play is the account of the trick by which the philosopher-king outwits the Cabinet. The gaiety is the clash of temperaments among the quarrelling ministers. The charm is the skill, courtesy and sweet temper with which the king smooths them down. There is an interlude in the middle of the story in which the king visits the tempestuous lady whom everyone supposes is his mistress. Like Shaw's own romantic affinities she is really a non-mistress. She is a recognizable portrait of Mrs. Patrick Campbell with whom Shaw used to have the same undignified scuffle as that which takes place on the stage, when Mrs. Patrick Campbell wanted to annoy Shaw's wife by making him late for tea.

*The Apple-Cart* has been successfully revived many times, and the phrase "Breakages Limited", meaning a too-powerful vested interest, has become part of the English language. It was Shaw's last great play. He wrote some more political and sociological ones, most of which were first performed at the annual Malvern Festival, *Too True to be Good, On the Rocks, The Millionairess, The Simpleton of the Unexpected Isles, In Good King Charles's Golden Days* and *Buoyant Billions,* but each one takes an idea which he had already used and deals with it rather less earnestly and more impatiently. They are dramatized fables rather than plays. From time to time one of them is revived, by amateurs or repertory companies or on television, when they do come alive as stories but suffer from having been too topical when they were written. Another generation will hardly remember the Hitler, Mussolini, Franco and T. E. Lawrence whom the original audiences were delighted to recognize in them. In *The Apple-Cart* Shaw came to the end of his greatest period as a dramatist and in fact as a writer.

### The Intelligent Woman's Guide to Socialism and Capitalism

Shaw wrote this between 1923 and 1926 when if he had continued to write plays instead he could have made a great deal of money. He was at the summit of his fame. But he wrote it out of the same earnest sense of duty he had given to his political-speaking activities when he was a Fabian and to the affairs of St. Pancras when he was a vestryman. This guide is his testament of Fabian socialism. It is chiefly about economics, which he considered the most important business of the civilized world, because he believed that only by Socialist economics could we banish poverty and the abolition of poverty must be the first aim of civilization.

It is a charmingly-written, easily-understandable treatise of the subject as it was seen by the early Fabians. Some of its conclusions are those of Shaw as an individual. He modified some of his ideas between the nineties and the nineteen-twenties. Parts of it are inevitably dated now. He sees the economic problem of Socialism as a black-and-white issue, a struggle between Labour and Capital, as Marx did. The class struggle, when he was writing, was more simply definable than it is now. All the same the book lasts on as a clear, logical and entertaining exposition of late-nineteenth and early-twentieth-century radicalism and gives the reader some idea of the way he must have amused and entertained and informed audiences when he was the most popular political lecturer of his day.

### The Black Girl in Search of God

In 1932 Shaw wrote this short book about a black girl searching through the various religious beliefs of man, looking for God. She is helped to come to terms with the fact that she cannot find Him, but must be content to know that He exists, by an old philosopher, representing Voltaire. He tells her that it is enough for her to fulfil His purposes without fully understanding them. She marries a free-thinking Irishman (otherwise Shaw himself) who tells her that he suspects that the Life Force is trying experiments, proceeding by a process of trial and error and not perfectly sure of its own aims yet.

When this book first appeared, it aroused considerably more indignation from religious authorities than it would today, after *Honest to God* and *Soundings* have opened the door to fresh ideas. But conventional churchmen picked on a point which was not the main issue. They were indignant that Shaw should suggest that God made mistakes. The curious thing about this criticism is that in the Old Testament stories the idea of God repenting that He had made man, and considering the alternative of scrapping the experiment altogether is part of the traditional theology.

Shaw, when asked exactly what this book meant, persisted that he did not really know.

### Everybody's Political What's What

Shaw wrote this collection of essays during his late eighties. It sums up the opinions of his lifetime and is useful as a reference-book to students of Shaw, though it says nothing that he has not said, more forcibly and entertainingly, elsewhere. If it had been the work of any other octogenarian, the reader would have to be impressed by its controversial and dynamic ideas. But Shaw had a lifetime of self-expression behind him and each theme can be found, more strikingly clothed in words and dramatic situations, in something he had already written. The subjects of these essays are topical, firmly embedded in the mid-twentieth century, and therefore many of them are already dated, in contrast to his plays about timeless subjects, such as the Life Force, and man's struggle with his conscience, and legendary figures like Joan and Caesar.

At this distance after his death, his view on the society of his own day is neither modern enough to be immediately relevant nor old enough to be seen in perspective. For instance to the reader brought up in the first decade of the welfare state, his arguments in favour of communal responsibility sound too obvious to be interesting, though future generations may be able to trace social history from them. Shaw himself thought that his personal views expressed in essay form were more important than his plays. But any current collection of his sayings invariably consists almost entirely of quotations from the plays themselves. It is as a dramatist that he takes his place among the immortals.

# Index